A Pre-Emancipation History of the West Indies

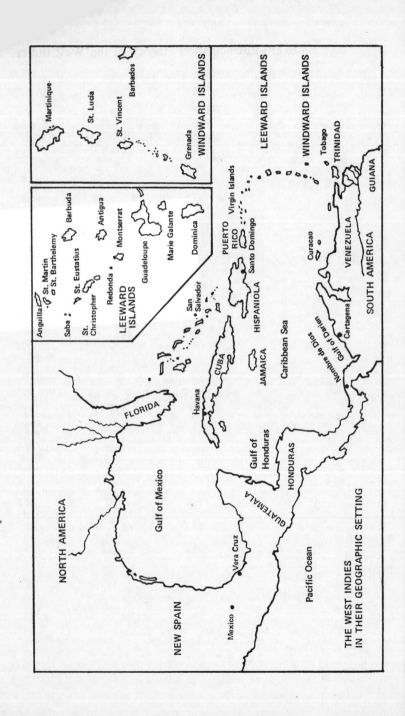

THE WEST INDIES
IN THEIR GEOGRAPHIC SETTING

A Pre-Emancipation History of the West Indies

Isaac Dookhan Ph.D

Lecturer in History
College of the Virgin Islands
formerly Head of History Department
Indian Education Trust College, Georgetown, Guyana

Longman Caribbean

Longman Group UK Limited,
Longman House, Burnt Mill, Harlow,
Essex CM20 2JE, England
and Associated Companies throughout the world

Carlong Publishers Ltd
PO Box 489,
95 Newport Boulevard,
Newport West,
Kingston 10,
Jamaica

LongmanTrinidad Limited,
Boundary Road,
San Juan,
Trinidad

First published by Collins Educational 1971
This impression published by Longman Group UK Ltd 1988
Fifth impression 1991

Produced by Longman Group (FE) Ltd
Printed in Hong Kong

ISBN 0-582-02804-3

Acknowledgment

The Examination Questions on pages 151 to 156
have been reproduced by permission of the
University of Cambridge Local Examination
Syndicate and the University of London, School
Examinations Department.

Contents

Preface   7

1. Discovery and Rivalry   9

Conditions in Europe which lead to the voyages of Columbus 10   *The results and consequences of Columbus' voyages* 13   *Spanish assertion and defence of its monopoly in the West Indies* 14   *Reaction of European nations to the growth of Spanish power and the actions they took to weaken it* 16   *Extent of Spanish West Indian decline in the 16th century* 18   *The progress of European colonisation in the West Indies to the end of the 17th century* 19   *Reasons for Spanish neglect of the Lesser Antilles* 21 *Reasons why Englishmen settled on St. Christopher first* 22   *Importance of the buccaneers in the West Indies* 23   *The role of the Dutch in the 16th and 17th centuries* 25   *Spanish efforts to prevent foreign incursion into the West Indies in the 17th century* 28   *The Dutch Wars* 30   *(a) The First Dutch War, 1652-1654* 30   *(b) The Second Dutch War, 1665-1667* 31   *(c) The Third Dutch War, 1672-1678* 33   *The extent to which the wars between European powers in the West Indies were due to West Indian factors* 34   *Effects of the War of the Spanish Succession (1702-1713) on the West Indies* 36   *Effects of the War of Jenkin's ear and the War of Austrian Succession (1739-1748) on the West Indies* 37 *The effects of the Seven Years' War (1756-1763) on the West Indies* 38 *Effects of the American War of Independence (1776-1783) on the history of the West Indies* 39   *Effects of the French Revolutionary and Napoleonic Wars (1793-1815) on the West Indies* 41

2. The Plantation System   44

Why early English and French settlers made their homes in the West Indies. Some difficulties they experienced 45   *Reasons why early English and French settlers concentrated on tobacco cultivation* 46   *Changeover from tobacco to sugar. The part played by the Dutch* 48   *Consequences of large-scale sugar production in the West Indies* 49   *The layout and organisation of an ordinary West Indian sugar plantation* 51   *The cultivation of sugar-cane and the manufacture of sugar* 53   *Reasons for planters' dissatisfaction and grievances in the 18th century* 54   *Causes for the decline of British plantation agriculture* 56   *The West India Interest* 58

3. Slavery   61

The types of labourers used in the West Indies before 1838 62 *Participants in the African slave trade* 64   *Description of the slave trade as it occurred in Africa, the Middle Passage and the West Indies* 66

Social grouping during slavery: group differences 69   *Living and working conditions of slaves on an estate* 71   *The West Indian Slave Laws with special reference to 'Code Noir'* 73   *Slave Protests* 76   *The Revolution in St. Domingue, 1791* 79   *Arguments used for and against slavery* 82   *The struggle for the abolition of the slave trade* 83   *The aims of amelioration: its limited success* 86   *Factors which aided the abolitionists and emancipationists* 87   *Provisions of the Act of Emancipation* 89   *Emancipation in the French West Indies* 90

4. The Apprenticeship System   93

The aims of apprenticeship and how far they were realised 94   *The role of the Stipendiary Magistrates and the difficulties they encountered* 95   *An assessment of the work of the Stipendiary Magistrates* 97   *The end of apprenticeship* 99   *Problems facing the West Indies after 1838* 100

5. Colonial Government   104

The Government of the Spanish American Empire 105   *Defects and merits of Spanish Colonial Government* 108   *British Colonial Government under the Lords-Proprietors* 109   *The Old Representative System* 111   *The reasons for conflicts between British West Indian Assemblies and the Colonial Office in the 18th century* 113   *The introduction of Crown Colony Government* 114   *Advantages of Crown Colony Government* 116   *Disadvantages of Crown Colony Government* 117   *The Morant Bay Uprising and Crown Colony Government in Jamaica, 1865-1866* 118   *Government of the French West Indies* 120

6. The Religious Denominations   124

The role of the Church in the Spanish American Empire 125   *Functions of the clergy and missionaries in the British Colonies* 128   *Attitude of the planters towards the Anglican clergy in the British colonies* 130   *Attitude of the planters towards the missionaries in the British Colonies* 131   *Difficulties of the clergy and missionaries in the British Colonies* 132

7. The Mercantile System   136
The Spanish system of trade 137   *Reasons for the British Navigation Acts of the 1650s and 1660s* 139   *The principal features of the British Mercantile System* 140   *Effects of the Navigation Acts* 142

List of Short Note Topics   146
A Select Bibliography   149
Examination Questions   151
Index   156

Preface

The aim of this book has been to produce a text of sufficient depth for examination purposes, which, at the same time, caters for the understanding of students and promotes an adequate grasp of the subject.

This study has been divided into seven parts for convenience of treatment and to highlight the main trends in West Indian history. These are, Discovery and Rivalry; The Plantation System; Slavery; Apprenticeship; Colonial Government; The Religious Denominations; The Mercantile System. In keeping with current trends and the state of research findings, the emphasis on the different parts has been varied. The sub-divisions indicate the main issues involved. These have been worked out on the basis of a series of questions submitted to students over a period of time for private study, classroom discussion and essay topics.

The treatment of the subjects in the text varies. In some cases answers are given in the form of essays, as they should be presented for examination. In other cases, because of limited space, the essential points only are enumerated. In the first instance, the student gets an indication of how to organise thoughts; and, in the second instance, he is introduced to the art of preparing notes for himself on subjects other than those treated here and in which he may be interested.

The use of this text should not preclude study of regular textbooks used in schools. There are obvious advantages of comprehension and of detail that can be acquired from wide reading.

Because this text has been prepared to suit particular examination requirements, some subjects have had to be left out. Nor was this considered the proper place to deal with the history of individual colonies such as Cuba, Jamaica and St. Domingue, except when particular events there, illustrative of West Indian feeling and action, make it necessary. Such instances as the revolution in St. Domingue in 1791 and the Morant Bay Uprising of 1865, fall into this category. Moreover, in the West Indies, dominated by Spain, England and France, the lesser nations, Sweden, Denmark and the Netherlands (at least after the destruction of Dutch supremacy in the latter half of the 17th century) have had to be relegated to a background position so far as treatment of their colonial affairs is concerned.

So far as the colonies of Spain, England and France are concerned, the problems of selection have to be seen from other levels. The most obvious is that of language. Besides, it is natural for English-speaking students to concentrate their study on the system which has the most significance to their understanding and way of life. Hence the greater emphasis on the history of the British West Indies.

Within these limitations, however, an attempt has been made to introduce students to the main subjects, trends and events in West Indian history, more or less before 1838. To this end, even though syllabuses did not deem it quite necessary, some subjects have been introduced to achieve continuity and completeness of study. Examples of these are the sections on Dutch Wars, Crown Colony Government, Problems facing the West Indies after 1838, and the Morant Bay Uprising in 1865.

Included at the end of the text is a select bibliography of the major works consulted in the preparation of this volume. In addition, lists of revision questions have been included at the end of the individual chapters, as well as at the end of the book. These questions at the end have been selected from actual examination papers for the General Certificate of Education, Ordinary Level. They concentrate on the main topics in West Indian history and should prove an invaluable guide to study.

Finally, it should be mentioned that the author has incorporated in this work many of his own findings in West Indian history, which were the product of years of research from original sources. He has made full use of relevant suggestions and factual information obtained from students in the course of teaching. The work has certainly been enriched thereby.

College of the Virgin Islands
January, 1971

1. Discovery and Rivalry

Although they were separated from Europe by thousands of miles of unknown seas, the West Indies, in their discovery and settlement, were an out-thrust of the ideas and achievements of Europeans in the 15th and 16th centuries. The early history of the West Indies can best be understood from a study of the rivalry which existed between European nations desirous of establishing colonies in, and partaking of, the wealth of the region.

The value of the islands in terms of mineral wealth, tropical plantation agricultural products, employment of Europeans and a training ground for naval personnel, made them particularly desirable as overseas possessions. As such they aroused the jealousy and envy of colonising nations. The various West Indian islands were not only the pawns in international politics, but the seas surrounding them constituted a main theatre of naval warfare between those European nations contending for the right of possession over them.

Because of their comparative inaccessibility and poverty, the West Indies remained for more than a quarter of a century after their discovery the exclusive property of Spain, unmolested by foreign intervention. But as soon as the wealth of the New World became evident and the possibilities of trade showed themselves, there was a steady and increasing invasion by the nationals of other European countries. The challenge to Spain's monopoly took several forms. Smuggling, piracy and privateering destroyed its exclusive trade policy, while the establishment of settlements on the yet unsettled islands of the Leewards and Windwards destroyed its territorial monopoly over the region.

Spain had based its monopolist claims to the West Indies on the grounds of prior discovery and the rulings of the Pope through papal bulls. But the inability of Spain to defend its stand by force of arms, and the rejection of the authority of the Pope in Europe as a result of the Reformation, enabled other maritime European nations to assert their rival argument to their claim to part of the West Indies, namely, that of effective occupation. Military victory over Spain in Europe enabled them to assert their rights and to establish their claim to trade and settle in the West Indies.

The acquiescence of Spain, however grudging and reluctant, to foreign presence in the West Indies, did not result in peaceful settlement and development of the islands. The increasing prosperity of the West Indies especially after the introduction of sugar-cane, resulted in war among the three major colonising nations, England, France and the Netherlands. At first the conflict raged between England and France on the one hand and the Netherlands on the other, in an attempt by England and France to remove the Dutch from serious competition in the trade and commerce of their respective colonies. With the Dutch disposed of, the English and French turned against each other. From the later 17th century to the early 19th century the conflict raged almost incessantly as they sought to acquire each other's colonies.

1. Conditions in Europe which led to the voyages of Columbus

The voyages of Columbus towards the end of the 15th century cannot be seen as isolated events but as a continuation of the voyages of Europeans overseas. By the time of Columbus, Europe was already undergoing a process of expansion as exemplified by the achievements of the Portuguese earlier in the 15th century. The legacy of exploration was significant in stimulating the Spanish ventures but other factors were equally important in promoting Columbus' voyages.

By the 15th century, Europe was experiencing fundamental social and political changes. European feudal society was disorganised and 'over-mighty' lords were challenging the authority of kings. It became obvious that if order was to be maintained and the state preserved, the authority of the king had to be maintained. This could only happen if the king had the means at his disposal to maintain his supremacy. In order to effect this, trade had to be expanded and new sources of wealth secured. Accordingly, new rulers gave active encouragement to the exploration of new lands overseas.

The 15th century, also, was a time of growing nationalism in Europe. There was a tendency to stress national differences and to forget the international concept of Christendom. National individuality and identity were strengthened by 'national' wars. National kings sought to maintain their power against the power of the Pope and

European Emperor and to project the status of their new states. To do this, the acquisition of new territory suggested itself.

Again, in the 15th century, Europe was experiencing what is termed the Renaissance or Rebirth of Learning. The Renaissance did two things: it emphasised the power of the individual and of individual achievement; and, it focused men's attention on the world outside Europe, challenging them to explore it. The development of printing enabled new ideas and facts to spread widely and the growth of schools and universities allowed more people to benefit from the new knowledge. Improvements in navigational science, for example charts and the compass, and improvements in ship-building, enabled Europeans to venture farther overseas to challenge accepted concepts and beliefs.

At the same time, there was an increasing demand in Europe for products from Asian countries including essential foodstuffs such as spices and peppers, luxury goods such as silks and perfumes, drugs and jewels. Following their conquest of Constantinople in 1453, the Turks gradually extended their control over the lands bordering the Eastern Mediterranean. As a result, the old trade routes between Europe and Asia by land and by sea were impeded by the excessive tolls that were exacted by the Turks. In addition, a controlling monopoly over certain branches of the Asian trade was held by Genoese and Venetian merchants. In order to by-pass the obstacles to profitable trade with Asia imposed by the Turkish impediment and the Italian monopoly, it was necessary that Western Europe should find alternative trade routes.

Apart from these commercial factors, other developments in Europe prompted the voyages of Columbus. Thus, the study of geography and astronomy was being applied to the problems of practical navigation. The art of ship-building and the skill in handling ships were being improved. Firearms and particularly naval gunnery were developed to take care of hostile native peoples if necessary. Besides, there was an increasing preoccupation with technical problems among Europeans and their mastery of a wide range of mechanical devices. These developments coincided with a new outburst of courage, discipline and organising ability, and with the zeal of a crusading spirit.

Europeans were affected to a large extent by a missionary zeal to convert heathens to Christianity and at the same time to end the power of the Muslim Turks. Associated with this aim, was their desire to find the Utopia or perfect society to provide the pattern for their own institutions and which they believed could be found overseas.

Finally, the system of European government at the time allowed for a greater measure of individual incentive and a broader basis of private participation. As such, competing ideas and interests sustained a great creative effort. It went a far way towards arousing the initiative which led to the voyages of Columbus.

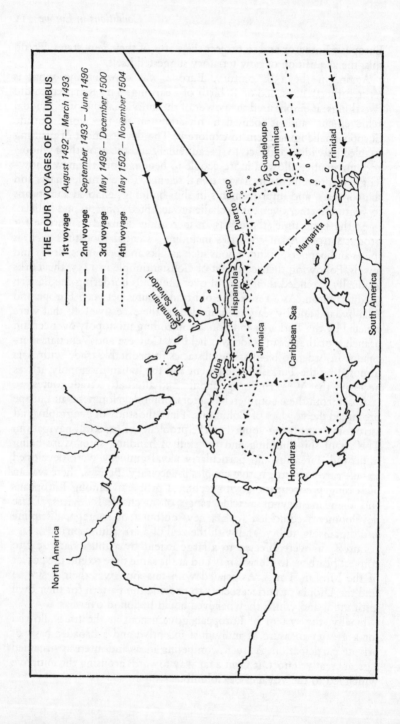

THE FOUR VOYAGES OF COLUMBUS

1st voyage	August 1492 – March 1493
2nd voyage	September 1493 – June 1496
3rd voyage	May 1498 – December 1500
4th voyage	May 1502 – November 1504

North America

Guadeloupe
Dominica

Trinidad

Puerto Rico

Margarita

Guanahani
(San Salvador)

Hispaniola

Jamaica

Caribbean Sea

South America

Cuba

Honduras

2. The results and consequences of Columbus' voyages

Although Columbus was probably not the first European to reach the New World, the discovery of the West Indies is attributable to him. He revealed to Europeans the existence of lands which had been inhabited for centuries before, though they were practically unknown.

The history of the West Indies can be said to date from the time of their discovery by Columbus in the sense that, henceforth, that history was recorded and given more precise definition.

Altogether Columbus made four voyages to the West Indies with the assistance of King Ferdinand and Queen Isabella of Spain who were anxious to compete with Portugal for overseas trade and conquests. On his *first* voyage (3rd August, 1492—15th March, 1493) Columbus discovered the Bahamas, Cuba, and Hispaniola. On his *second* voyage (25th September, 1493—11th June, 1496) he discovered Jamaica and Puerto Rico in the Greater Antilles. In the Lesser Antilles, he discovered Dominica, La Desirade, Marie Galante, Guadeloupe, Monsterrat, Antigua, St. Christopher, Nevis, St. Martin, St. Croix and other Virgin Islands, the Isle of Pines off the coast of Cuba, and several other unimportant small islands. On his *third* voyage (31st May, 1498—December, 1500) Columbus discovered the mainland of South America, Trinidad, Grenada, St. Vincent, the rich pearl fisheries of Margarita and Cubagua, and probably Tobago. Finally, on his *fourth* and last voyage (9th May, 1502—6th November, 1504) Columbus added St. Lucia, Martinique and the mainland of Central America to his previous discoveries.

With the discovery of the West Indies by Columbus began the systematic exploration of the lands of the New World by other European discoverers. The West Indies often provided the necessary base for the exploring thrust farther west.

With the discovery of the West Indies, also, began a period of international dispute between Spain and Portugal with regard to the right of possession to the newly discovered lands. In order to effect a settlement, the matter was referred to Pope Alexander VI, the recognised international arbiter. The result was a series of papal bulls. The first two gave to Spain all lands discovered by Columbus. The third provided for a line of demarcation drawn north to south 100 leagues west of the Azores and Cape Verde Islands, and stipulated that lands and seas west of this line should be the Spanish sphere of exploration and influence. These bulls constituted the legal basis for Spanish monopolist claim to the lands of the New World. In 1494, the Pope's decisions were ratified by the Treaty of Tordesillas between Spain and Portugal. But the Treaty shifted the line of demarcation 270 leagues farther west, thereby giving Portugal the right to Brazil.

For a number of reasons the Spaniards settled only on the larger islands of the West Indies, namely, Hispaniola, Cuba, Jamaica and Puerto Rico, where they could at once satisfy their lust for precious metals and their inclination to rear cattle. Neglect of the smaller islands lead to their eventual settlement by other European nations.

The Spanish monopolist claim to the West Indies soon came to be challenged by other maritime European nations, most notably, England, France and the Netherlands, who were desirous of sharing the wealth of the region. However, it was not until the 17th century that these nations were able to establish any settlement or colony of their own in the West Indies.

European settlement in the West Indies began a new era in the lives of the native Indians. The Spaniards soon began to enslave them and to subject them to gross indignities which were alien to their nature. They died in large numbers partly from overwork in the gold mines and partly from the various diseases introduced by the Europeans. From this time began their gradual depletion which was soon to end in their almost complete extinction from the West Indies.

It was one of the triumphs of Columbus that he not only found a way across the 'Sea of Darkness' to the American mainland, but also worked out the best outward and homeward routes for sailing ships travelling between Europe and the Caribbean.

3. Spanish assertion and defence of its monopoly in the West Indies

With the discovery of the West Indies by Columbus, Spain claimed an exclusive monopoly to the region. The monopoly extended both to territory and to trade. In the 15th century, two fundamental principles governed the right of possession to newly discovered lands. These were firstly, prior discovery which included the authorising and financing of voyages of discovery and, secondly, papal authority sanctioning the right of possession. These principles were for a long time asserted by Spain in support of its claim to the West Indies.

The division of the New World between Spain and Portugal was accepted as final by these two countries. But it was rejected by all other countries interested in colonisation.

In opposition to the Spanish arguments of prior discovery and papal decree giving right of possession, other maritime European nations desirous of securing foot-holds in the Caribbean, forwarded their counter-argument of occupation, that is, the establishment of settlements, as the only effective basis of right of possession. In turn, this assertion was vigorously opposed by Spain so long as Spain possessed the military power to do so.

Spanish arguments of prior discovery and papal decree were the theoretical bases of Spanish claims. These would have been useless unless they could have been effectively supported by military measures. Accordingly, forts and fortresses were erected at strategic points in the major islands to guard the most important cities and harbours such as Santo Domingo, Santiago de Cuba, Cartagena, Havana, Vera Cruz, and San Juan del Puerto Rico. A Windward Squadron was organised to patrol the seas at regular intervals to intercept trespassers and prevent any disruption of the Spanish trade or territorial monopoly. Individual islands, Hispaniola, Cuba and Puerto Rico, also instituted patrols by 'guarda costas' for the same purpose. Ships engaged in illegal trade were to be seized, and any settlements commenced were to be destroyed. Crews and settlers were to be arrested, tried and imprisoned.

The Spanish system of colonial administration played an essential role in the preservation of the monopoly. The bureaucratic centralisation of authority and the appointment of the highest officials, both secular and ecclesiastic from among Spaniards born in Spain, ensured the enforcement of government policies, the preservation of Crown privileges, and the non-evasion of Spanish monopoly. In the Council of the Indies, the Spanish Crown had a powerful instrument to direct the affairs of Spanish America. Its all-pervading authority ensured that colonial matters were rigidly controlled. The Royal officials, whom it appointed, for example, the Viceroys and audiencias, and the system of checks and balances, served to guarantee that orders were enforced.

Among the offices established to administer colonial affairs was the House of Trade (Casa de Contratacion). In keeping with its policy of exclusion, regulations were introduced to confine the trade of the West Indies to Spain. This meant that colonists could only legally buy what they required from Spain and sell what they produced to Spain, and then only to selected Spaniards. All other persons desirous of trading with the Spanish colonists had to be properly licensed. The establishment of a separate institution to regulate trade and to enforce trade laws indicates that Spain was unwilling to tolerate any participation of foreigners within its exclusive domains.

The Catholic Church also served to maintain Spanish monopoly in the West Indies. The Church was an essential arm of government. By its teachings it sought to make the native population accept Spanish domination. The Inquisition was used to discourage foreign Europeans from entering and establishing themselves in Spanish territory. By its control over teaching, the Church could exclude foreign ideologies which might be harmful to Spanish presence in America. And finally the Church provided the spiritual buttress to the secular arm of Spanish colonial government.

4. Reaction of European nations to the growth of Spanish power and the actions they took to weaken it

The West Indies had special attraction for non-Hispanic European nations. As a source of Spanish wealth, the region aroused their fear and envy. The wealth obtained by Spain was used to finance its European wars and the extension of its supremacy in Europe. The fear of conquest and the resolve to prevent it were uppermost in the minds of European statesmen. In order to boost their own power, non-Hispanic nations sought to share in the wealth obtained in the New World. The West Indies were specially desirable as plantation colonies from which tropical plantation products could be obtained and to which European manufactures could be sold. Possession of lands in the West Indies, moreover, could provide the bases from which the Spanish mainland colonies could be attacked.

The Spanish monopolist claims to the West Indies on the grounds of prior discovery and papal decree were not accepted by the non-Spanish maritime European nations. Their rejection of the authority of the Pope during the period of the Reformation in the 16th century signalled an attack on Spain as the bastion of Roman Catholicism in Europe. To weaken Spain, they decided to attack it at the source of its wealth.

Spain's restrictive trade regulations proved irksome to the Spanish colonists in the West Indies and encouraged their violation. The high prices demanded for Spanish manufactures and the comparatively low prices offered for colonial produce were direct consequences of an exclusive trade policy. Moreover, commodities needed could not always be obtained in sufficient quantities. This was a severe hardship since the colonists often depended on European supplies to provide the barest necessities of life. In addition, in order to undertake agriculture the colonists soon came to demand negro slaves but supplies fell short of demand. The colonies, therefore, lacked adequate means for steady social and economic development.

Some attempt was made by Spain to defend its West Indian possessions by means of forts and other fortifications, by a mobile navy and by guarda costas. Some attempt, too, was made to defend trade by the adoption of a convoy system. These attempts, however, were inadequate to resist any concerted attack by a determined enemy and failed to prevent their incursions into the West Indies.

Spanish theoretical arguments were rejected by rival European nations. The counter-argument of effective occupation was used. This meant that the establishment of settlements was a necessary prerequisite to the right of possession. On the basis of this argument, non-Hispanic nations claimed the right to settle on islands which had not been occupied by Spain. Pressures of war in Europe forced Spain to make valuable concessions to its rivals such as were made to France in 1559, to England in 1604, and to Holland in 1609, touching on their right to trade in the West Indies.

Even before the treaty concessions, the Spanish monopoly had already been breached in the West Indies. Smugglers were attracted by the valuable trade that could be transacted with disaffected colonists. Isolated coasts and secret coves off island plantations were visited by these smugglers with cargoes of foodstuff and merchandise. When the shortage of labour following the failure of the native Indians to provide an adequate supply, directed attention towards negro slave labour, the importation and sale of black Africans became an important line of the smugglers' activities. The Portuguese were the first smugglers since their possession of Brazil facilitated their presence in the West Indies under cover of transacting trade with that colony. They were followed by the English and the Dutch. The activities of the Englishman, John Hawkins, should be noted. Between 1562 and 1568, Hawkins organised four trading voyages to the Caribbean in which he traded cloth, general merchandise and slaves, for sugar, hides and silver. He laid the line along which illegal trade was transacted by those who came after him.

Smuggling was only one of the ways by which non-Hispanic nations invaded Spanish monopoly in the West Indies. Their indulgence in privateering and piratical activities were others. Privateers operated under the direct sanction of European governments which provided them with letters of marque, which were special commissions given by a country at war to armed vessels belonging to private owners so that they could carry on the operations of war against the enemy. Pirates operated on their own initiative. The activities of privateers were confined to periods of European wars involving Spain. Pirates operated at all times. The Spanish convoy system tended to protect many of the treasure fleets sailing from the New World to Spain, but isolated vessels became the prey of the sea-rovers. Similarly, the concentration of heavily armed forts around the larger colonial cities to a large extent protected them against attack. However, as the sacking of Santiago de Cuba and Havana by the privateering raids of Francois le Clerc and Jacques de Sores in 1554 shows, even the well-fortified cities were susceptible to invasion and capture. Generally, raids were directed chiefly at smaller, relatively unprotected settlements along the coasts. The raids of Sir Francis Drake need special mention since Drake evolved a coherent plan for attacks against Spanish settlements in place of the series of hitherto unco-ordinated raids. Drake was an illegal trader turned pirate. Among his most outstanding achievements were the sacking of Nombre de Dios in 1572, and of Santo Domingo and Cartagena in 1585. Drake was not always successful, as witnessed by his defeats at San Juan del Puerto Rico and Panama in 1595, but he did great damage, took much booty, and weakened the fighting power of Spain.

The establishment of settlements in the West Indies by non-Hispanic European nations occurred in the 17th century. By then, Spain had been weakened to the point of being unable to defend its monopoly by force of arms.

Spanish neglect of the Lesser Antilles paved the way for other European countries to exercise their principle of effective occupation. After unsuccessful attempts in the mainland territory of Guiana, the English established their first settlement in 1624 in St. Christopher in the West Indies. There, they were soon joined by the French. By the mid-1630's, islands adjacent to St. Christopher were settled—Nevis, Anguilla and Montserrat, by the English, and Martinique and Guadeloupe by the French. These were plantation colonies. The Dutch who were more interested in trade, established island entrepots in Saba, St. Eustatius, Curacao and St. Martin, all strategically situated for trade with the surrounding colonies.

By the early 17th century, Spanish monopoly had been irreparably breached. Spanish decline in Europe and its inadequate defence of the West Indies made Spain unable to maintain its theoretical monopolist claims to the region in the face of determined resolve by other European nations to share in the wealth and territory of the region. Early breach of the trade monopoly was made by smugglers; the Empire suffered systematic weakening by the pirates and privateers; and the territorial monopoly was subsequently destroyed by planter-colonists who were attracted by the gains to be obtained in Europe from the fruits of West Indian agriculture.

5. Extent of Spanish West Indian decline in the 16th century

During the 16th century Spanish monopolist claims to the West Indies were severely challenged by opposition from smugglers, privateers and pirates. Non-Hispanic European governments gave their blessings to such enterprises. The aim was to reduce Spain both financially and territorially. Destruction was considerable and losses great but by the end of the century the Spanish Empire in the Indies appeared intact even though scarred.

The attacks of raiders did not seriously hamper the development of Spain's colonial empire or drain it of its wealth. The plunder carried off was a small fraction of the produce of the Spanish colonies. Population increased rather than decreased and there was a steady enlargement of governmental machinery. The building of towns continued despite the destructions. Reliable figures show that by 1600 there were over

200 cities in Spanish America with a total population of over 150,000.

No nation, except Spain held territory in the West Indies during the second half of the 16th century, in spite of all the fighting. Spanish efforts were effective in excluding foreigners from settling in the region. The persistent raiding by French and English adventurers undoubtedly weakened, but it did not destroy or reduce the extent of the Spanish-American Empire.

Destruction of Spanish possession was not always significant. Many of the towns were undefended, without forts, guns or garrisons, and the citizens could hardly be expected to put up a strong resistance to the desperate men who attacked them. In many cases, also, there was little to defend and the raiders seldom got much booty at the smaller towns, especially as the townsfolk often had warning of a coming raid and were able to hide their valuables and escape into the interior. Even when such a town was burnt the damage done was comparatively unimportant as the flimsy houses could easily be rebuilt.

However, if the looting and destruction of small towns were of little importance and scarcely more than pinpricks, it was otherwise where the capture of large fortified cities like Santo Domingo, Cartagena and San Juan, and the heavy losses inflicted on Spanish shipping were concerned. Apart from the material losses suffered, these were serious affronts to the dignity of Spain. That such things were possible proved to those interested that the Spanish colossus was weakening and that it was not strong enough to defend the vast territories to which it laid claim. European nations envisaged the possibility of establishing themselves in the West Indies. The time was near at hand when they were to found colonies there in defiance of Spain.

6. The progress of European colonisation in the West Indies to the end of the 17th century

With the discovery of the West Indies by Columbus after 1492, Spain asserted an exclusive right to the entire area. Spain itself established settlements only on the larger islands of the Greater Antilles namely, Hispaniola, Cuba, Puerto Rico and Jamaica, leaving the Lesser Antilles unoccupied.

The first permanent Spanish settlement was established by Columbus on the northern coast of Hispaniola, on his second voyage in 1493. This settlement was removed a few years later to a more favourable location, the site of Santo Domingo.

During the early years of the 16th century, Spanish settlement was begun on Cuba and, to a lesser extent, on Jamaica and Puerto Rico. The colonists raised cattle, tobacco and sugar-cane, and mined gold in modest quantities. Hispaniola and Cuba served as bases for expeditions sent out to explore the mainland of America and to settle it. With the discovery of gold and silver there in large quantities, the Spanish West Indies lost much of their population to the mainland colonies, and the islands assumed the character of coaling stations and supply depots.

Some mention must be made of Trinidad at the other end of the Antillean chain. In 1530, Spain made an abortive attempt to settle it. Thereafter the island remained in practical oblivion until 1595 when Antonio de Berrio was appointed governor and colonisation became more firmly established. Even so, because of Trinidad's isolated position, the colony was neglected throughout the 17th and 18th centuries.

For nearly forty years no other Europeans seriously challenged Spanish interests in the Caribbean. Some interlopers did come in peace time to trade with the settlers. It was from the 1530's that privateers and pirates raided Spanish colonial harbours either as private enterprise or in furtherance of national political and military aims. The objectives were to deny to Spain the means of making war and to exploit the islands. By 1600, however, no settlements had been made in the West Indies by non-Spaniards.

The turn of the 16th century witnessed great changes in the West Indies as Spain suffered military reverses in Europe. Much against its will, Spain was forced to give up its claim to unoccupied lands and to trade in the New World by treaty agreements with France, England and the Netherlands. The 17th century was the period of settlement.

England and France were chiefly interested in establishing plantation colonies. The first permanent English settlement in the West Indies was on St. Christopher (St. Kitts) by Sir Thomas Warner in 1624. There they were joined by the French under D'Esnambuc shortly after, and both groups shared the island until the English expelled the French during the War of Spanish Succession. Englishmen also settled on Barbados in 1627 after Captain John Powell had taken possession of it for the English Crown in 1624. In 1625 the English and Dutch established a settlement on St. Croix, in 1628 the English settled on Nevis, and in 1632 on Antigua and Montserrat. In 1635, the French established themselves on Martinique and Guadeloupe.

In the 17th century, the Dutch led Europe in shipping and commerce and this explains their emphasis on colonies as trading entrepots. The islands on which they settled in the 1630's—Curacao, St. Martin, Saba and St. Eustatius—served as centres for trading and smuggling. In addition, Curacao provided salt for the fishing fleets of the Netherlands, as did Aruba and Bonaire.

Jamaica, which was the least developed of the Spanish islands, was captured in 1655 by an English expedition under Admiral Penn and General Venables sent out by Oliver Cromwell to attack the Spanish

Empire in the Indies. The larger Windward Islands—Dominica, St. Lucia, St. Vincent and Grenada—remained unsettled to the end of the 17th century. Early attempts to colonise them by the English and French (for example, the English in St. Lucia between 1638 and 1641) had been repulsed by the large numbers of warlike Caribs who lived there. Settled development on these islands did not in fact take place until after 1763 when the islands became British possessions. Even so their existence was very unstable.

The second half of the 17th century, after the introduction of large scale cultivation of sugar-cane, was a period of increasing prosperity for the Lesser Antilles. This aroused the greed of the European nations who sought to expel rivals and to possess the islands for themselves. The Three Dutch Wars (1652–1654; 1665–1667 and 1672–1678) and the War of the Augsburg League (1689–1697) were fought with West Indian ambitions. Already islands began to pass from one European nation to another as the fortunes of war ebbed and flowed.

In the 18th century when the West Indian colonies became more prosperous, the islands figured more prominently at the conference table of European nations met to conclude treaties of peace after the many European wars then fought.

7. Reasons for Spanish neglect of the Lesser Antilles

The discovery of the West Indies by Christopher Columbus was accompanied by Spanish settlements in the islands. But Spaniards did not establish settlements on all the islands discovered. Rather there was a marked concentration of effort on the larger islands such as Hispaniola, Cuba, Puerto Rico and Jamaica which make up the Greater Antilles. Alternatively, the smaller islands of the Lesser Antilles were neglected. There was nothing haphazard in the action of the colonists. Their concentration on the larger islands was dictated by the motives of colonisation, by the geography of the region and by the desire for survival.

A dominant motive of Spaniards coming to the West Indies was the desire for gold and silver so that they could become rich quickly. Evidences of gold in the Greater Antilles had been obtained by Columbus on his first visit to the islands, and the subsequent discovery of gold and silver ensured that these islands would secure maximum attention. No evidence of precious metal was obtained in the Lesser Antilles.

In terms of agriculture, the small islands possessed no advantage over the large islands. Instead, the bigger acreage of the latter would easily have made them the favourite of those seeking to engage in agriculture. Besides, whatever natural products the islands produced could be obtained more easily and in greater quantities in the large than in the small islands.

Compared with the Greater Antilles, the Lesser Antilles were more densely wooded, the forests often extending to the shore of the islands. In addition, the small islands were comparatively more mountainous, or alternatively, had a smaller percentage of flat land than the large islands. These geographical characteristics had their corresponding disadvantages. Forests made penetration and the establishment of settlements extremely difficult while the mountainous nature of the islands posed the additional problems of easy internal transportation and communication. Forests and mountains combined made the small islands unsuitable for cattle-rearing which was an essential occupation of the early Spanish settlers.

The question of security in the Lesser Antilles made the Greater Antilles favourites. The small islands were infested with fierce, warlike Caribs in contrast to the more peaceful and tractable Arawaks of the large islands. Carib raids against settlers would have been more potent and destructive in view of the existence of mountain fastnesses: these would have facilitated the escape of the Caribs and prevent their easy dislodgement.

Inter-island communication was effected by means of sailing ships. Thus the direction of prevailing winds was of importance. The geographical position of the Lesser Antilles made the approach to them from Spain across the Atlantic Ocean before the prevailing North-east Trade Winds comparatively easy. But Spanish colonial administration was concentrated in the large islands. To sail back from the Lesser Antilles to the centres of Spanish power to the north-west was difficult.

Spanish neglect of the Lesser Antilles made the islands vulnerable to other European nations who desired to establish colonies in the West Indies. When this was achieved in the early 17th century, the way was paved for further incursion into Spanish monopoly in the New World.

8. Reasons why Englishmen settled on St. Christopher first

The same primary motives which led other Europeans overseas, namely the desire for wealth and markets, the need for tropical products and for territory, led English pioneers to the New World. Although the desire to cultivate the soil was not among the aims of the early colonisers, the first settlement to be permanently established was in the nature of a plantation colony. After unsuccessful English attempts to found colonies on the mainland of South America between 1602 and 1620, the first successful settlement was established in St. Christopher (now called St. Kitts) in 1624 by Sir Thomas Warner.

This settlement was a consequence of the expulsion of the English from the Amazon by the Portuguese in 1620. There was nothing haphazard or accidental in Warner's proceedings. Apart from the neglect of the island by the Spaniards and its availability for settlement, several other good reasons prompted his decision.

Warner had made a reconnaissance of the islands on his way home to England from the Amazon venture and had entered into friendly relations with the chief of the St. Christopher Caribs, named Togreman. From this observation, he concluded that the island would best suit his intention to plant tobacco.

For the purposes of colonisation and agriculture, Warner needed an island which could provide a safe anchorage, a fertile soil, a healthy climate, and a good water supply. Not all the islands of the Leeward group satisfied these requirements. For example, Barbuda, though larger, was rocky and seemingly barren, while Antigua was considered unhealthy and deficient of water.

Larger islands such as Guadeloupe, Martinique, St. Vincent, Dominica and St. Lucia, were avoided because Warner knew that his force would be small at the outset and that those islands contained many more Caribs than did St. Christopher. There, also, the savages had the additional advantage of mountain fastnesses from which it would have been difficult to dislodge them.

From the point of view of safety from external enemy attack, the island was considered satisfactory. The outward bound Spanish fleets from Europe commonly passed through the Windward Passage, disliking the more intricate navigation of the Leewards. After his Amazon experiences, Warner must have put privacy high on the list of advantages of a prospective plantation.

There is no record that Warner knew of Barbados, which was superior to St. Christopher in terms of potential as a plantation colony. All the various factors being considered, therefore, Warner could feel justified in making St. Christopher the scene of the first English settlement in the West Indies.

9. Importance of the buccaneers in the West Indies

One of the most important influences on West Indian history during the 17th century was the buccaneers who contributed to a considerable degree to the weakening of Spanish control in the Caribbean and to the protection of English, French and Dutch settlements.

The buccaneers consisted of fugitives from the law, religious and political refugees from different countries, escaping white indentures, retired sailors, and small planters who had been displaced during the sugar revolution. They were all hardy and tough. From being at first hunters of wild cattle and traders in 'boucan' in Hispaniola, they drifted into a life of piracy when they were dislodged from their normal occupation by the Spaniards. In time they came to operate from two main centres: Tortuga, an island off the north coast of Hispaniola, and Port Royal in Jamaica after 1655 when England conquered the island from Spain. The first centre was dominated by the French, and the second centre by the English. Other smaller centres were in the Gulf of Honduras, along the Mosquito Coast of Nicaragua, and sections of Central America where Spanish authority scarcely existed and Buccaneers found little resistance.

The buccaneers were ruthless and reckless men. Though they had no political allegiance, they tended to gather in national groups and reserved the right to exempt ships of their own nation from attack. It was not difficult for maritime European nations interested in acquiring colonies in the West Indies to draft the buccaneers into their fighting forces. To them were issued letters of reprisals in times of war to attack enemy possessions. They were made the instruments of national policy in the fight to wrest territory from Spain. They were thus absorbed into the colonial system. Often they proved to be unreliable allies since they were attracted by gain no matter from where it came.

The buccaneers carried on the 'unofficial' war between Spain and other European nations which had raged continuously in the West Indies for more than a century. It was not until 1670 by the Treaty of Madrid by which Spain agreed to recognise the right of Britain to possess colonies in the West Indies, that Britain undertook to suppress buccaneering. As far as the French were concerned, official buccaneering was encouraged just at the time when the English were trying to stamp it out. By the Treaty of Ratisbon in 1680, however, France agreed to restrict its buccaneers. The Treaty of Ratisbon marked the official end of buccaneering. The actual end naturally took some time to achieve and it was only with the Treaty of Ryswick in 1697 that the age of the buccaneers came to an end.

The effects of the buccaneers in the West Indies can be summarised:
  (i) During the Dutch wars of the 1660's the buccaneers were almost the only fighting men available to Britain in the West Indies. They were used as the striking force by sea.
 (ii) The activities of the buccaneers in Tortuga led to the eventual acquisition of St. Domingue by France.
(iii) The participation of the buccaneers in the third Dutch War (1672–1678) contributed to the bankruptcy and collapse of the Dutch West India Company and enabled the French to enforce a commercial monopoly in their own West Indian colonies.

(iv) The toll taken by the buccaneers was a heavy one. For instance, during the period extending from 1655 to 1671, they sacked eighteen cities, four towns, and nearly forty villages. From 1660 to 1685, the period of buccaneers' greatest success and most savage reputation, the depredations of the buccaneers against the Spaniards amounted to an estimated 36 million U.S. dollars excluding the loss of more than 250 merchant ships and frigates.

(v) Though buccaneers assisted Britain to establish its right to possess colonies in the West Indies, they indirectly injured English trade as much as they injured Spanish navigation. For instance, their depredations against Spanish ships aroused the anger of Spanish colonists who withheld their trade from English traders; it became difficult for English merchants to absorb the trade and riches of Spanish America through the peaceful agencies of treaty and concession.

(vi) The development by Spain of the Greater Antilles as productive settlements was impossible while the buccaneers continued to receive support. This, in large measure, accounts for the fact that the cultivation of sugar took such a late start in the Spanish colonies.

(vii) The attacks of the buccaneers combined with the trading activities and naval attacks of the English, French and Dutch, and the disorganised state of the Spanish colonial system, were effective in bringing about the overthrow of Spanish monopoly in the West Indies.

(viii) In the long run, even the British colonies suffered from the activities of buccaneers. For example, through buccaneering Jamaica lost many of its bravest men, lowered the moral tone of the island, and retarded the development of its natural resources. Between 1668 and 1671, an estimated 2,600 men were lost to buccaneering. In the British West Indies generally, many white colonists turned their attention to buccaneering instead of to agriculture.

10. The role of the Dutch in the 16th and 17th centuries

The expansion of Dutch power in the Caribbean was influenced by the desire and need to extend Dutch commerce outside Europe. This meant intruding on lands claimed and controlled by Spain, and by Portugal also if Brazil is included. To engage in overseas trade the Dutch had to engage in overseas war. Their success in trade and war gave them their overwhelming influence in the Caribbean by the middle of the 17th century.

Dutch activities in the Caribbean can be divided into four phase which coincide with the great period of expansion of the United Netherlands. The first phase extending from 1585 to 1597 was exploratory and entirely commercial; the second phase from 1598 to 1608 was one of growth in commerce; the third phase from 1608 to 1621 was marked by the establishment of colonies; and the fourth phase after 1621 witnessed tremendous expansion and consolidation of interests.

Dutch commercial thrust outside Europe was first determined by the need for salt for the fishing and dairy industries, for domestic consumption and for re-export. Supplies from the Iberian peninsula were insufficient during the Anglo-Spanish War (1585–1604). This war made Dutch ships liable to seizure, and in order to avoid this, supplies were sought elsewhere. In 1585 Dutch ships landed at the Cape Verde Islands for salt. These voyages continued and as opportunities arose, cargoes of other commodities such as sugar, wines and dyewoods were procured. From there the thrust extended to the Canaries, Madeira and eventually Brazil. By 1595 Dutch ships were appearing at Cumana on the Spanish Main, and at Santo Domingo in the West Indies. In 1598, the first Dutch ships explored and traded along the rivers of Guiana between the Orinoco and the Amazon.

According to the bulls issued by Pope Alexander VI in 1493, Dutch entry into the New World was illegal. Dutch trading activities in the Caribbean, therefore, were in the nature of smuggling enterprises. Between 1598 and 1608 an average of twenty-five Dutch ships a year were engaged in smuggling with the Spanish colonists and Indians of the Spanish American mainland, Cuba and Hispaniola. European merchandise was bartered for hides, sugar, ginger, pearls and pieces of eight. From around 1606, negro slaves were added. The most important branch of Dutch navigation in the Caribbean, however, was salt-hauling at Punta del Araya in Venezuela. Possibly more than 100 vessels were engaged in the trade annually.

In November, 1606, an attempt was made by Spain to rout the Dutch from the Caribbean. Twenty Dutch salt ships were destroyed off Araya by a Spanish fleet under Fajardo, and their crews killed or imprisoned. This attack only strengthened Dutch exertions and invited their retaliation. In 1603, 130 Dutch privateers had sailed into the Atlantic, and in 1607, the Dutch Admiral Jacob van Heemskerck inflicted a severe defeat on Don Juan Avila in the Bay of Gibraltar. In 1608, however, peace negotiations were commenced and finalised the following year.

The Twelve Years' Truce did not halt Dutch encroachments upon the Spanish Empire. It is true that the salt trade at Araya was not revived, and that smuggling was conducted on a moderate scale. But the Dutch followed a policy of exploring trading opportunities and establishing plantation colonies in areas unoccupied by Spain and

Portugal. For instance, between 1610 and 1611, colonisation was undertaken in Guiana, from the Essequibo to the Amazon Rivers. Some Dutch factories, established earlier, were transformed into settlements. In 1615, settlements were founded in Cayenne, the Wiapoco and the Amazon, and in 1616 the first permanent colony was established in Essequibo. These proved successful.

The end of the Twelve Years' Truce in 1621 and the beginning of renewed fighting between Spain and the Netherlands coincided with the formation of the Dutch West India Company to give power and direction to Dutch offensive in the Caribbean. The Company became the instrument of national commercial and military policy. Dutch exclusion from Araya, expulsion from the Amazon and failure to capture Puerto Rico, were answered by a military success against Bahia in Brazil. It was the Dutch West India Company's privateering successes in the Caribbean between 1626 and 1629, which generally weakened Spanish resistance.

With fourteen ships in 1626 – 1627, Piet Heyn sailed to Bahia and seized twenty-three loaded sugar vessels; in 1627 Van Uytgeest captured a rich Honduras galleon; in 1628 Pieter Ita captured two Honduras galleons, and Piet Heyn with thirty-one ships and 4,000 men captured an entire Spanish silver fleet, a feat hitherto unaccomplished. Its cargo was sold for 15 million florins wherewith the Company paid its debts and planned a major attack against Brazil. In 1630, Hendrick Loncq with sixty-four ships and 8,000 men captured Pernambuco; during the next seven years, four northern provinces in Brazil were taken, and Dutch occupation of Curacao, Bonaire, Aruba and St. Martin in the West Indies was begun. Dutch naval victories in Europe and Brazil reinforced the Caribbean conquests. In October, 1639, a combined Spanish-Portuguese armada of sixty-seven vessels and 24,000 men was defeated by Admiral Tromp in the English Channel, and in January, 1640, another Spanish-Portuguese armada of eighty-six ships and 12,000 men was defeated by a Dutch West India Company fleet of forty-one vessels.

The Dutch victories broke Spanish monopolist resistance in the Caribbean and paved the way for the infiltration, virtually unmolested, of other European nations into the New World. In 1629, for instance, under cover of Piet Heyn's victory, 500 Puritans from England established themselves in Massachusetts Bay. Even before this, in 1624, the English and French had begun the settlement of St. Christopher from where they spread to the other Lesser Antilles.

Dutch contribution to non-Hispanic settlement did not extend only to military exploits and protection. Their overwhelming superiority in capital resources and ships over all other European nations facilitated the consolidation of the non-Spanish West Indian settlements as plantation colonies. Under the aegis of the Dutch, sugar was introduced into the English and French islands: the Dutch provided necessary credit and bought the produce of the infant colonies. Finally, they furnished the colonists with European manufactures and foodstuffs which their superior mercantile navy enabled them to supply at lower cost than elsewhere.

11. Spanish efforts to prevent foreign incursion into the West Indies in the 17th century

The wealth of the Spanish Caribbean attracted the attention of European nations who wished to share it. Contraband traders, pirates, privateers, buccaneers and settlers all tried in their separate ways to seize a part of the Spanish claim.

Spanish resistance to foreign aggression to about 1586 was slight. Until then neither the Crown revenues nor Spanish sovereignty in the West Indies were greatly endangered by the prevalent sacking of small towns and villages and the seizure of coastal shipping. Spain was more preoccupied in European struggles and spared little effort for the American colonies. Protection there was left to local militias formed from among the colonists. Spain was largely concerned with imposing severe penalties against intruders and the provision of annual convoys for the fleets. It also sought to prevent foreigners from learning the sea routes to the West Indies and operated a spy system to furnish warnings of attack. The obvious defences, namely, the maintenance of forts and garrisons in the settlements and the use of the fleets against sea marauders, were little regarded. Diplomatic interchange remained fruitless so long as Spain's forces were weak. At peace conferences following war, the West Indies were generally unmentioned, and even periods of peace witnessed continued attacks against the Spanish Indies.

Beginning in 1586, with the sacking of Santo Domingo and Cartagena by Drake and Hawkins, Spanish resistance stiffened. For about fifteen years a consistent plan was followed. Major ports like Havana, San Juan de Ulua, Puerto Rico and Puerto Bello were fortified and garrisoned with regular troops. Coastguard fleets were developed and other squadrons strengthened or renewed. A Windward Squadron for the protection of the whole Caribbean was created in 1598. The strength of Spanish resistance was shown by the repulsion of Drake and Hawkins in 1595 from Puerto Rico and Panama.

Spanish power of resistance, however, was short-lived. Economic deterioration of Spain, the defeat of the Spanish Armada in 1588, and the weakness of Spanish monarchs after the death of Philip II in 1598, all contributed to cause dwindling resources and lack of energy. After peace had been made with France at Vervins in 1598, with England at London in 1604 and with the Netherlands at Antwerp in 1609, there was a disastrous lack of steady policy for America. Work on forts stopped and garrisons went unpaid for months at a time and became discontented. The Windward Squadron fell to ruin. By the early 17th century, Spanish activity consisted only of attempts to end the widespread contraband trade by severe treatment of those captured, or by removing its American opportunities.

The remainder of the 17th century witnessed bursts of great activity punctuating years of slothful decay. The sporadic outbursts of energy were due largely to the stimulus of some special danger or disaster in America. The end of the Twelve Years' Truce with the Netherlands in 1621 resulted in the strengthening of the Antilles with garrisons and arms. The great period of foreign colonisation in the 1630's and 1640's accounted for other activities. The English assault on Santo Domingo and seizure of Jamaica in 1654 and 1655, respectively, led to widespread construction of defences. The results were cumulative as time passed. By the last quarter of the 17th century most harbours important for trade or military strategy possessed strong forts and fair garrisons. A small squadron formed of a poor type of ship and stationed at Cartagena was inadequate but it persisted until 1665 when it was combined with the newly founded Windward Squadron. The convoy ships attached to trading fleets, as well as naval detachments infrequently despatched from Spain on special missions were furthermore quite active.

By these means Spain achieved far more than is commonly realised. Given anything like equal terms, its ships won at sea as often as they lost, and Spain frequently repulsed attacks made with great force against its settlements. No foreign colony was established in the West Indies without serious danger of attack or dislodgement by a Spanish force. If Spain never had the strength to recoup its chief losses like Jamaica and Curacao, and lacked resources to hold such important re-conquests as Tortuga, St. Kitts and Santa Catalina, yet such losses of small islands were minor and relatively unimportant compared with the large wealthy territories retained in South and Central America and in the West Indies. If by the Treaties of Munster with the Netherlands in 1648, of Madrid with Britain in 1670 and of Nymwegen with France in 1678, Spain agreed to recognise foreign presence (that is, colonies and trade) in the West Indies, it was because it recognised the virtue in acceding to the inevitable. Spain was steadily declining while other nations were growing stronger. Some concession could avoid the collapse of the entire structure. In its endeavour to prevent further incursions into Spanish territorial monopoly, Spain adopted a policy of appeasement and compromise rather than one of complete aggression. Such policy did not mean wholehearted toleration. Spanish attacks against foreign colonies in the 18th century attest to Spain's desire to rid the West Indies of intruders.

12. The Dutch Wars

There were three Dutch Wars after the middle of the 17th century. In West Indian history the results of these wars were important and far-reaching and special emphasis needs to be placed on them.
Certain basic causes lay at the foundation of these wars.
(i) Trade rivalry. The Dutch because of their greater power or ability to give cheap credit and transport facilities and to offer higher prices in their markets for West Indian products, had secured for themselves markets which should have been available to England and France. The wars were attempts to break the Dutch predominance in West Indian trade.
(ii) The desire for power and prestige. This was especially so with England during the Commonwealth and Protectorate period of Cromwell when a nascent nationalism found expression in such measures as the Navigation Acts of 1650 and 1651. This developed into a desire for supremacy and commercial superiority in the Caribbean. When Colbert became Minister of Finance in France in the 1660's, he aimed to increase French influence in Europe. One way to do this was to break Dutch commercial supremacy.

Apart from these basic causes which were common to all the Dutch wars, there were other specific causes which were peculiar to each individual war.

The First Dutch War, 1652–1654

Following the passing of the English Navigation Act in October, 1650, the Dutch tried in June, 1651, to negotiate mutual free trade with England. But the negotiations broke down. Rather, under the influence of its merchant-advisers the English Parliament proceeded to pass the restrictive Navigation Act of October, 1651. This Act was aimed directly at the Dutch who held almost a monopoly of the maritime trade of the world. When the envoys of the United Provinces re-opened the negotiations early in 1652 and appealed to the English Council of State for the suspension of the Navigation Act, they met a direct refusal. England wanted its colonial trade for itself. War resulted.

The fighting of the First Dutch War was almost entirely confined to European waters. In the Caribbean there was generally a tacit understanding between the Dutch and the English to preserve neutrality and to continue pursuit of their own local interests.

Despite this feature of the war, however, its general results with regard to the West Indies should not be overlooked.

(i) It broke the commercial links that bound the English and French planters to the Dutch merchants and traders.

(ii) With the English cruisers scouring the English Channel and the North Sea, it was impossible for the Dutch merchant ships to continue their old trade with any regularity and English merchants could take full advantage of the 1651 Navigation Act.

(iii) Sugar poured into the London warehouses and English manufactures were carried back to the islands in steadily increasing volume.

(iv) Planters who had previously sought loans in Middelburg, or in France, now found their backing in London and the channel of trade was permanently diverted.

(v) Commercial pressure had compelled the Netherlands to sue for peace, and for the first time the effects of the stranglehold that a maritime power could exert upon a mercantile nation were shown fully in international affairs.

(vi) The Treaty of Westminster, April, 1654, saw the restoration of amicable relations and mutual recognition of possessions held at the date of the Treaty. The Dutch were also compelled to acquiesce in their exclusion from the trade with the English colonies and the serious limitation of their commercial opportunities which that involved.

(vii) Cromwell, falling in with the opinion of the majority of his Council, determined to launch a surprise attack in force against the Spanish West Indies which seemed to offer inexhaustible opportunities of plunder. It was the beginning of his 'Western Design'.

(viii) The war marked the crucial turning point in English policy. Henceforth, English statesmen aimed at extending England's control over more of the fertile West Indian islands.

The Second Dutch War, 1665–1667

The first step that led unmistakably to another Dutch War was taken in 1663 when King Charles II of England despatched Captain Robert Holmes with a well armed squadron to the African Coast to protect English claims against interference with their slave trade. Circumstances inimical to English interests, for example, Dutch hostility and their influence over local chiefs, forced Holmes to disobey instructions and undertake hostilities. In 1664, he seized and occupied the Dutch factories at Goree, Cape Verde, Cape Coast Castle, etc. and took several ships he found trading for slaves. Dutch reprisals were thus provoked.

To preserve the last remnants of their monopoly of the slave trade, the Dutch fitted out Admiral de Ruyter with a strong squadron. He arrived in Guinea waters in January, 1665, reoccupied Goree and expelled the English from various of their posts on the Gold Coast. He confiscated many English-owned slaves. Sailing across the Atlantic, Ruyter attacked Barbados and raided the English Leeward Islands. He captured the ships lying in the harbours of Montserrat and Nevis and completely destroyed their cargoes. The Second Dutch War resulted. In 1666, the French joined the Dutch against England. The war was marked by widespread destruction and by the backward and forward shuffling of the various colonies as they were captured and retaken in turn. For example, early in the war, Saba and St. Eustatius were captured by the English, but the latter was recaptured the following year. In 1666, the French took St. Christopher, Antigua and Montserrat.

The results of this war were as important as those of the first:

(i) The struggle had been more bitter than any other previous hostility between maritime European nations in the West Indies. Because France had joined the Dutch against England and had driven the English from St. Christopher, its legacy was acute hatred between the English and French colonists on the island where earlier there had been mutual tolerance and respect.

(ii) During the war the Dutch had lost all of their colonies except Curacao, and most of their shipping. Most of the old channels for illicit trade with the Spanish colonies were blocked or severed. In the West Indies, the war marked a further decline in Dutch commercial supremacy.

(iii) All but two of the English and French colonies lost nearly all of the prosperity they had achieved in 40 years.

(iv) Only Jamaica and Hispaniola seemed to have escaped the ravages of the war and seemed to benefit from the influx of fugitives.

(v) The war demonstrated the unreliability of using buccaneers as instruments to further English national policy.

(vi) The Treaty of Breda (July, 1667) which ended the war, marked a definitive distribution of colonial possessions in the islands between the rival powers. England got New Netherlands and regained her position in St. Christopher; the Dutch got Surinam; and the French got Acadia, Tobago and St. Eustatius. Until the mid-18th century, there was little change in the ownership of the 'sugar islands' and planters could consolidate their position without foreign interference. But no systematic adjustment was really made by the Treaty to the English and the Dutch differences.

(vii) The question of trade was not settled but remained the main preoccupation of English and French statesmen.

(viii) The Dutch hold was weakened but they were still the greatest traders in the Caribbean. Another war was necessary to drive them from the ranks of the great powers.

The Third Dutch War, 1672–1678

This war actually lasted from 1672 – 1678 but it was divided into two periods: 1672 – 1674, which saw fighting between England and France on the one hand and the Dutch on the other; 1674 – 1678, when fighting took place between France and the Dutch.

The Anglo-Dutch War was the outcome of dissatisfaction over the results of the Second Dutch War. Louis XIV was determined to crush Dutch commercial supremacy in the French West Indies.

In February, 1674, after the Dutch had made a blistering attack against Montserrat and Nevis and had succeeded in sweeping French commerce from the West Indies, England came to an agreement with the Netherlands and signed the Treaty of Westminster. England was influenced by Spanish efforts to persuade the Dutch to co-operate with her in reconquering Jamaica, and also by the danger to English trade to the Spanish colonies. The Dutch were also anxious for peace. According to the Treaty:

(i) English precedence at sea was admitted and a heavy indemnity was paid by the Dutch.

(ii) England accepted Dutch predominance in the trade of the East Indies, which they regarded as of vital importance.

(iii) There was to be a mutual restitution of all conquests except St. Eustatius and Saba, taken by the English Governor, Stapleton. The Dutch did not want the immediate return of these as they would be open to French attack. They remained English until 1678.

The war broke Dutch trading supremacy in the British West Indies, and the Treaty marked the final break between Britain and France. Henceforth, conflict in the West Indies was primarily between these two nations. The Netherlands and Spain were pushed in the background.

The peace of Westminster left France alone to deal with the Dutch. The highlights of the next four years were (a) the attack of De Ruyter on Martinique which proved so costly that he returned to Europe, and (b) D'Estree's attack on Curacao in 1677 which failed so miserably—the fleet being completely wrecked on a coral reef—that D'Estree also returned to Europe.

In August, 1678, two treaties were signed at Nymwegen between France and the Netherlands. It was agreed that each should retain all places then in its possession. France retained the Dutch ports on the

Senegal, thereby obtaining access to negro slaves there. When the French refused to recognise an 'open door' for Dutch commerce in the West Indies, the commercial supremacy of the Dutch in the region was finally broken. Indications were given as early as 1674 when the Dutch West India Company became bankrupt.

13. The extent to which wars between European powers in the West Indies were due to West Indian factors

The 18th century was characterised by a series of wars among the European nations which possessed territories in the West Indies. These wars included the War of the Spanish Succession (1702–1713); the War of Jenkin's Ear and the War of Austrian Succession, (1739–1748); the Seven Years' War (1756–1763), the War of American Independence (1776–1783); and the French Revolutionary and Napoleonic Wars (1793–1815). The excuse for these wars was usually some European quarrel but for both general and specific reasons, the West Indies contributed to the outbreak of hostilities.

The reason for much of the bitterness and widespread fighting between European nations in the 18th century was the rival struggle for colonies and trade. The West Indies were among the most prosperous of European possessions overseas. The colonies of one European nation aroused the greed and jealousy of another. War offered them the opportunity to seize each other's colonies. Some like Britain, were impelled by 'a mood of greedy and truculent imperialism.'

Other reasons dominated European action. In Europe, the wealth of the West Indies was used to provide the sinews of war. For countries which sought dominance in Europe, and for those who sought to prevent domination, West Indian wealth was the means by which their differing aims could be achieved. For Britain which experienced an Industrial Revolution after the middle of the 18th century, the colonies were valued to the extent that they promoted industrial growth. For all Europeans, colonies were desired as markets for manufactured goods and as sources of raw materials. Sugar colonies were especially valued since sugar was in high demand. In 1763, for instance, Britain contemplated retaining the captured French islands of Martinique and Guadeloupe and giving Canada to France in return.

Specific causes of West Indian origin leading to war were not evident in the War of Spanish Succession (1702–1713) between Britain and the Netherlands on the one hand and France and Spain on the other. It stemmed rather from the ambitions of Louis XIV of France who desired to unite the thrones of France and Spain under a single dynasty. This posed a threat to the security of Europe, and other nations moved to counter the danger.

The War of Jenkin's Ear between Britain and Spain, which merged into the War of Austrian Succession (1739–1748) in which France became involved was fought expressly for West Indian ends. The main cause of war between Britain and Spain was Spanish intransigence in the West Indies. The sporadic expressions of hostility against British colonies and colonists since the Treaty of Utrecht in 1713, the seizure of British vessels by Spanish 'guarda costas' and the cruel treatment of their crews, and the reprisals and counter-reprisals which ensued, led to hatred of Spain in Britain. The publicity given to the incident of Jenkin's ear, allegedly severed by Spaniards in the West Indies in 1731, increased the war fever and provided the excuse for an almost inevitable conflict. The war between Britain and France was governed by the bitter rivalry between two existing sets of sugar colonies. The French West Indian Islands, larger and more fertile, competed successfully with the British Islands in the production of cheap sugar and in the trade with Europe and British North America. War offered the British an opportunity to cripple French sugar production since they could not defeat France in open competition.

The Seven Years' War (1756–1763) was fought mainly between Britain and France. Spain joined France against Britain in 1762. Between the British and French in the West Indies there was great friction for some time before war broke out. Thus in 1753, a French force seized Turks Island and captured Bermudan vessels loading salt there. The main cause for friction in the West Indies was, however, the reluctance of the French to evacuate the neutral islands of Dominica, St. Lucia, St. Vincent, and Tobago in accordance with the Treaty of Aix-la-Chapelle in 1748. Spain's entry in the war stemmed partly from disputes with Britain over the question of the logwood camps in British Honduras and the Mosquito Coast of Nicaragua. It stemmed also from Spain's dissatisfaction with the execution of the Treaty of Commerce of 1750 with Britain, with the British 'Rule of War of 1756' by which any Spanish ships suspected of having touched at a French colonial port was liable to seizure, and, finally, with the British threat to annex the neutral islands in the Windwards, to which Spain made some shadowy claim.

The last two wars, the American War of Independence (1776–1783) and the French Revolutionary and Napoleonic Wars, (1793–1815) were not due to specific West Indian events, though the West Indies became involved as colonies of participating European nations. In the first war the rebellious American colonies were joined by France and Spain since these nations were dissatisfied with the outcome of the Seven Years' War and sought revenge. In the second war the conflict was mainly between Britain and France; but Spain, the Netherlands and Denmark joined France against Britain for part of the conflict.

14. Effects of the War of the Spanish Succession (1702–1713) on the West Indies

(a) The fortunes of the West Indian islands fluctuated as naval supremacy in the Caribbean passed from one side to the other. Unlike the Leeward Islands, neither Barbados nor Jamaica suffered during the war, although there were small raids by privateers on the latter when a few slaves were carried off.

(b) In spite of the alliance between France and Spain, the Spanish authorities in the West Indies did not sympathise wholly with their allies; and though French escorts for Spanish treasure fleets were accepted as a matter of necessity, Spain resented the position of France as the senior partner.

(c) Attempts were made by the British colonial governors and naval commanders to drive a wedge between the French and Spaniards, and trade was opened with those Spanish colonies whose governors were accommodating. But these governors were removed by the Spanish Government and the British efforts were unsuccessful.

(d) Whatever their attitude towards the French, the Spaniards never changed their hostility to the British and they treated all prisoners with great brutality.

(e) By the Treaty of Utrecht in 1713, British military and naval successes were rewarded by acquisitions of territory, including the former French part of St. Kitts, and by the award to the British of valuable trade concessions, including the 'Asiento' contract for the supply by a British company of 4,800 slaves a year to the Spanish colonies for thirty years, a contract which had previously been held by the French since 1702. The Spanish sovereign further undertook never to dispose of any of his American territories to another nation.

(f) It was agreed that an annual trading vessel 'a ship of 500 tons' from Britain should visit the Spanish colonies. This vessel might be accompanied by a tender carrying stores and that British factors might reside at Havana and at the principal ports on the Spanish mainland. There was much truth in Lord Acton's famous statement that the British 'acquired . . . in addition to the Asiento, the right of trading in the possessions of the House of Bourbon—in fact, the commerce of the world.'

(g) The over-all effect was to create further inroads into Spanish trading rights in the West Indies.

15. Effects of the War of Jenkin's Ear and the War of Austrian Succession (1739–1748) on the West Indies

(a) In the war between Britain and Spain, Admiral Vernon's initial success in capturing Puerto Bello and destroying its fortifications was not repeated. The great force sent out under Ogle and Cathcart to join him suffered from too ambitious orders and divided counsel. Havana was deemed too strong to be taken. Cartagena, where the galleons lay, was chosen as the first object, but the combined naval and military attacks on Cartagena and afterwards on Santiago de Cuba, were both failures. On the other hand, the English took many prizes and dislocated the normal lawful trade of Spanish America. Only one treasure fleet reached Spain and no galleons or 'flotas' sailed during the war. The Puerto Bello galleons were never again restored. The trade had to be carried either by single 'register ships' or by foreign smugglers. The smugglers thrived by war as their government intended they should and the British Government explicitly ordered Vernon to do his best to protect and convoy English trade with the enemy's colonies.

(b) The war between Britain and France was a different affair. It was governed not by desire to acquire new territories or new trades. War offered Britain an opportunity to cripple French sugar production. Naval activity was almost confined to cut off the trade of the colonies, to starve them of provisions and slaves and to prevent them from selling their sugar.

(c) The Treaty of Aix-la-Chapelle ended war in 1748.
  (i) No reference was made to the claim by Spain to the right to search British ships for contraband.
 (ii) The British right to the 'asiento' was reconfirmed.
(iii) All conquests were to be restored and in accordance with this arrangement, the forts on Roatan were destroyed and their settlers removed. But as the British settlements on the Belize River and the Mosquito Coast had not been formally annexed, their existence was ignored and their anomalous position was unchanged.
(iv) The neutralisation of Dominica, St. Lucia, St. Vincent, and Tobago was confirmed, and the British and French undertook to remove all their nationals from these islands which were to be left to the Caribs.

(d) The British imperial structure like the Spanish, creaked under the stress of war, but for all the British islands, war was the guarantee of prosperity. War had incidental disadvantages such as **privateering** losses, and high freight and insurance rates which offset war-time rises in the price of sugar. But war crippled the commerce of the productive French islands, it raised national anti-French feeling, and it caused people in Britain to shelve the economic question of the merits of British dependence on British-grown sugar. War, or the constant possibility of war, was to the advantage of the British West Indies, and no one in England doubted that the West Indies were worth fighting for.

16. The effects of the Seven Years' War (1756-1763) on the West Indies

(a) Trade suffered considerably from the raids of privateers.

(b) Until the beginning of 1759 there were no serious hostilities in the West Indies except that St. Bartholomew was captured by British privateers in 1757. After 1759 some minor naval actions were fought.
  (i) In May, 1759, a joint British force under Commander John Moore and Brigadier-General John Barrington captured Guadeloupe. The islands of Marie Galante, Desirade, Les Saintes and Petite Terre surrendered soon afterwards.
  (ii) In June, 1761, another joint British force under Commander Sir James Douglas and Lord Rollo captured Dominica.
  (iii) In February, 1762, Admiral Rodney took Martinique. Soon after, St. Lucia and Grenada capitulated.
  (iv) In August, 1762, a large British expedition under Admiral Sir George Pocock and General Albemarle captured Havana.

(c) The blockade of the French coast by British fleets had prevented adequate naval assistance being sent to the French colonies, all of which, except St. Domingue, had fallen to the British. The capture of Martinique deprived the French of their principal West Indian base for privateers while a large portion of the Spanish navy had been lost at Havana. The British navy was supreme at sea and behind this shield the British West Indian colonies were safe.

(d) By the Treaty of Paris in 1763:
  (i) Britain restored Martinique and Guadeloupe to France but retained Canada.
  (ii) Of the former neutral islands it was agreed that France should have St. Lucia while Britain took Dominica, Grenada and the Grenadines, St. Vincent and Tobago.
  (iii) Britain agreed to restore Havana to Spain and to keep Florida in exchange.

(iv) Special arrangements were made regarding Central America—Britain was to demolish all fortifications, while Spain agreed not to molest British subjects engaged in cutting or transporting wood and to allow them to have dwellings and warehouses necessary for their work.

(e) British occupation of Havana, though only for one year, had lasting results. The port had been thrown open to unrestricted commerce, thereby creating renewed Cuban interest in trade, and Spain found it practically impossible to re-establish the old restrictions on trade. Moreover, during the British occupation, Freemasonry, which was to play a leading role in the revolutionary impulse of the next decades, entered Cuba.

17. Effects of the American War of Independence (1776–1783) on the history of the West Indies

(a) Many British West Indians sympathised with the cause of the Americans. Bermuda, indeed, sided openly with the rebels and supplied them with ammunition and vessels until the arrival of British troops in 1779 put an end to these irregularities. On the whole, however, the colonists remained faithful to Britain.

(b) It was not long after the outbreak of hostilities between America and Britain that American privateers began to capture British merchantmen in the Caribbean, and between 1777 and 1779 they even ventured to raid the Grenadines, burning houses and carrying off slaves, and to attack and cut out vessels at anchor in the harbours of Tobago and other islands. The British navy was generally too busy to deal with the privateers. The French, Dutch, and Danish islands offered accommodation to the American privateers who used their ports as bases.

(c) The entry into the war of France in 1778, and of Spain in 1779, led to international conflict in the West Indies. In September, 1778, the French captured Dominica, and later, in June and July 1779, they took St. Vincent and Grenada, respectively. Early in 1782, the French took St. Kitts, and a little later Nevis and Montserrat. Meanwhile, the Spanish had captured the Bahamas in 1781. The British replied by seizing enemy colonies also. St. Lucia was captured in late 1778. The use of Dutch ports by enemy vessels led to the British seizing St. Eustatius and the three Guiana colonies of Essequibo, Demerara, and Berbice in 1781. All were shortly afterwards recaptured by the French. British naval activities were climaxed by a resounding victory by Rodney over the French Admiral, de Grasse, at the Battle of the Saints in April, 1782. Together with the financial exhaustion of the French, and their enormous commercial and maritime losses, it led to the end of hostilities.

(d) The Treaty of Versailles was concluded in September, 1783. By it Britain restored St. Lucia and ceded Tobago to France. In turn, France restored St. Kitts, Nevis, Montserrat, Grenada and the Grenadines, St. Vincent and Dominica to Britain. Spain undertook to restore the Bahamas and, in Central America, agreed that the British log-cutters should be allowed to work within an area bounded by the Belize and Hondo Rivers, their safety being guaranteed by the King of Spain. The British in turn, agreed to demolish all fortifications erected in Central America and to allow no new fortifications to be built there.

(e) The effects of the war had been extremely serious even for the few British islands, Antigua, Barbados, the Bermudas and Jamaica which had escaped capture by the enemy. Before the war, the West Indian colonies had depended on North America for foodstuff and lumber. Not only was this trade cut off but American privateers preyed heavily on the other commerce of the islands, and when France and Spain joined the war conditions became worse. Freight rates and insurance rose sharply. There was considerable distress in the colonies and appeals for help were made from time to time. Prices of imports, especially corn, rose considerably while the prices of sugar and rum fell. A large number of slaves, dependent on imported foodstuff which never arrived, died of starvation. In addition, the colonists suffered from fear of invasion. The necessity for martial law, which involved extra taxation to maintain local militias and to build and equip fortification, imposed an added strain on the economy of the islands which they could ill afford.

(f) The American war established the independence of the rebellious colonies. But independence converted hitherto British colonies into a foreign state and placed America beyond the pale of the British laws of trade and navigation. The British West Indies could no longer trade legally with America. The stoppage of supplies imposed serious hardships on British West Indian planters and their slaves, especially during periods of drought and hurricane. Henceforth, colonists had to depend on Britain for more of their foodstuff and manufactured goods and as an outlet for their produce. This swing in trade was not always in their favour as was demonstrated by the French wars. The American war contributed to the economic decline of the British West Indian colonies.

18. Effects of the French Revolutionary and Napoleonic Wars (1793–1815) on the West Indies

(a) The war period, 1793 to 1815, was divided into two parts separated by the Treaty of Amiens extending from March, 1802 to March, 1803. In 1795 France was joined by Spain and this alliance continued until 1807, when Spain became an ally of Britain. In 1795, also the Netherlands joined France, while Denmark sympathised with the French cause. These associations affected the fortune of the West Indian colonies.

In 1793, the British captured Tobago, and in 1794, Martinique, Guadeloupe and St. Lucia. The two islands of Guadeloupe and St. Lucia were shortly afterwards recaptured by the French but St. Lucia was again taken by the British in 1796. In 1796, also, the Dutch colonies of Demerara and Essequibo were taken, and in 1797 Trinidad was captured from Spain. In April, 1801, the Danish West Indies were seized.

By 1801, the British were supreme in the Caribbean, with the French practically confined to Guadeloupe, and the Spaniards to Cuba and Puerto Rico. By the Treaty of Amiens all conquests were restored, except Trinidad which was ceded by Spain to Britain.

During the second phase of the war from 1803 to 1815, Britain was supreme in the Caribbean after Nelson's victory over the French at Trafalgar in 1805. By the end of 1810 all European colonies in the West Indies except those belonging to Spain, which was in alliance with Britain since 1807, were in British hands.

By the Treaty of Paris, Britain restored to France and Denmark all the captured colonies except Tobago and St. Lucia. The Netherlands ceded to Britain the mainland colonies of Demerara, Essequibo and Berbice.

(b) The wars led to economic disaster for the French colonies. This was due not only to the ravages of war but more so, to negro insurrections in 1795.

(c) For the British islands the long war brought an economic reprieve. Before the slave rising of 1791 in St. Domingue, that territory had been exporting nearly as much sugar as the whole of the British West Indies. Its removal from effective competition favoured the British colonies. The price of sugar in London rose from 54/3 a cwt. in 1792 to 69/2 in 1796. The price of coffee doubled in the same period. British colonial exports of both commodities greatly increased despite wartime increases in costs of production, freights and insurance, and despite the steady increase in duties on colonial produce. Cotton also reached record levels of production and price during the war. Until about 1810, cotton remained an important and profitable West Indian product.

(*d*) The disturbed state of the Spanish colonies and the British alliance with Spain after 1807, allowed an increase in trade with Spanish America, sometimes legal through free ports, but more often not. The Anglo-American War (1812–1814), and the self-imposed blockade of American ports, removed a dangerous competition to British colonial trade, the United States itself. British exports to Cuba, for instance, more than trebled during the two years of the war. Jamaica and Trinidad both profited greatly from this increase in Spanish-American trade between 1808 and 1815.

(*e*) War-time prosperity was only temporary. With the coming of peace, prices of sugar and coffee dropped, but duties remained to pay for the cost of the war. British West Indian sugar was once more confined to the British market, since it was driven from Europe by competition from beet sugar, and by competition from cane sugar produced more cheaply by newer and larger plantation colonies such as Cuba and Brazil who used slave labour. The French wars marked a further step in the economic decline of the British West Indies.

Conclusion

The growth of European nationalism and the emergence of 'national' kings, the rise of the Renaissance spirit with its questioning of accepted beliefs, improvements in navigational science and shipbuilding, the increasing demand in Europe for Asiatic foodstuffs and luxury goods, the need to find alternative trade routes to circumvent the problems of those which existed, and missionary zeal, all prompted the voyages of Christopher Columbus. A final incentive was given by the successes achieved by the voyages of the Portuguese.

The discovery of the New World by Columbus revealed to Europeans a new region to be exploited. It also resulted in international rivalry for the right of possession over the new lands. Spain based its claim to exclusive possession on the grounds of prior discovery and papal decree, and sought to defend its monopoly by the adoption of restrictive trade laws and the institution of a convoy system, the erection of forts and fortresses, the creation of a mobile navy, the introduction of 'guarda costas', and the establishment of a highly centralised system of colonial administration.

Spain's position in the New World was challenged by other European nations who claimed effective occupation as the criterion for possession. They undermined Spanish monopolist claims through the agency of smugglers, pirates, privateers, buccaneers, settlers and by military confrontations in Europe. Through the 16th century Spain did not suffer much loss, but by the end of the 17th century, other European nations were firmly established in the Lesser Antilles.

The second half of the 17th century witnessed the First, Second, and Third Dutch Wars, primarily between England and the Netherlands in order to remove the latter from effective competition in trade with the West Indies. The 18th century also witnessed a series of wars—the War of Spanish Succession (1702-1713), the War of Jenkin's Ear and the War of Austrian Succession (1739-1748), the Seven Years' War (1756-1763), the American War of Independence (1776-1783) and the French Revolutionary and Napoleonic Wars (1793-1815) primarily between Britain and France, for supremacy in the West Indies. The islands became the pawns in international politics.

The mineral wealth of the New World was at first the main attraction of Europeans, but with the settlement of the Leeward Islands which had no precious metals, the focus was on agriculture.

Revision Questions

1. What did Columbus achieve in the Caribbean?
2. How did other European nations interfere with Spanish trade in the West Indies and with what success?
3. Why were the West Indies considered valuable by Europeans?
4. How did Spain seek to keep the wealth of its empire to itself?
5. Why and how was Dutch commercial supremacy in the West Indies destroyed?
6. Describe the main events in the West Indies in the wars among European nations between 1702 and 1763.
7. In what ways were the West Indies affected by European rivalry in the region in the 18th century? Show how the islands changed hands.
8. What was the attitude of the British West Indians to the American Revolution? What part did the West Indies play in the war?

2. The Plantation System

Colonies were valued to the extent to which they contributed to the wealth and prosperity of the imperial power to which they were attached. Essentially, tropical colonies were held in order to provide the mother country with much needed products which could not be produced in the temperate climate of Europe.

Beginning in the form of individual ventures on small holdings, whether or not these were sponsored by wealthy European merchants and others, West Indian agriculture came eventually to be dominated by the plantation system. In short, small holdings gave way to large estates. This involved the change from a small-crop economy based on tobacco, cotton, coffee, cocoa and indigo, to an economy based largely on sugar-cane.

The production of sugar-cane for export was one of the most important influences on West Indian history. For instance, by increasing the wealth of the islands, it stimulated international rivalry and conflict, and caused the colonies to be brought under more centralised control by the imperial powers both in terms of trade regulations and direct political management. The introduction of negroes to work on the sugar plantations not only changed the racial composition of the island populations but gave much scope for missionary activities when the white colonists themselves did not respond favourably to their religious overtures. In the sense that sugar production influenced all aspects of life in the West Indies, it can be said that for the most part, the history of the West Indies is the history of sugar.

Reliance, more or less, on a one-crop economy could spell prosperity or doom for the producers concerned. The major regulating influence was the condition of the European market. If marketing opportunities were favourable, that is, if demand and prices were high, and if freight, insurance and other marketing costs were low, planters and their associates prospered. Alternately, when the conditions which promoted prosperity were reversed, depression ensued. This explains why the planting interests were always at pains to maintain a favourable market for their product in Europe.

Despite, or because of, the restrictions placed on West Indian trade and the continuous series of wars, West Indian agriculture flourished in the 18th century. In the 19th century, however, economic depression set in. The vital sugar markets declined under the competition from foreign cane and European beet sugar. The falling profitability of plantation agriculture had serious effects on West Indian history. When it became obvious that the islands had lost their previous importance as markets for manufactured goods and sources of raw materials, and looked rather for imperial financial assistance, European interest in them became diminished and the islands lapsed into insignificance as overseas possessions.

1. Why early English and French settlers made their homes in the West Indies. Some difficulties they experienced

Reasons for settling

These have to be seen within the context of the conditions in Europe which led Europeans overseas. Among the reasons which can be mentioned here are:

(i) Official encouragement from the English and French Governments who wanted to break the Spanish monopolist claims to the West Indies.

(ii) People sought to become wealthy; the promise of gold and silver opened the prospects of getting rich quickly.

(iii) Some were attracted by the gains to be had from illegal trade.

(iv) Many families who lost their properties through war in Europe decided to make a fresh start in the West Indies.

(v) Love of adventure led many young people to the West Indies who had no prospects in Europe. Piracy, privateering and buccaneering attracted many.

(vi) Some people wanted to escape religious persecution.

(vii) Unemployment in Europe drove many people overseas where there was hope of getting ownership of a piece of land, even if it meant serving a period of indenture at first.

(viii) Criminals and prisoners of war were transported to the West Indies where they were compelled to give forced labour before they obtained their freedom.

(ix) Some people were kidnapped and forcibly sent to the West Indies.
(x) Some came to claim inheritances and to assume possession.

Some difficulties experienced

(i) The Atlantic crossing in those days was a hazardous exercise for which few settlers were prepared. Many became ill or died during the voyage.

(ii) Food was sometimes scarce because of unreliability of supplies. Where importation of foodstuffs was concerned, shortage was due to poor transportation facilities and the depredations of pirates and privateers. Local supplies were hampered by natural disasters like drought and hurricane.

(iii) Lack of experience in tropical agriculture. Many settlers were unable to grow their own food, and had to depend on imported supplies.

(iv) Tropical diseases killed many. The noteworthy example of this was, of course, yellow-fever.

(v) The colonists faced rebellion from indentured servants and slaves.

(vi) There was little social life in the colonies; life was a struggle to exist against many odds; the amenities of contemporary European society were lacking to a large extent.

(vii) The people suffered from bad housing and uncomfortable accommodations until the increase in wealth made it possible for some of them to live grandly.

(viii) Few social services such as educational and medical facilities existed. There were few ministers of the gospels to cater for the religious needs of the people.

(ix) All were unaccustomed to the hot tropical climate which created problems of adjustment.

(x) The rough and heavily wooded terrain of the islands posed internal transportation and communication problems.

(xi) Dangerous insects, reptiles and other animals were a continuous nuisance.

(xii) The early settlers were troubled by frequent attacks from the war-like Caribs and the Spaniards both of whom sought to dislodge them.

(xiii) Administration of the colonies was unsettled and the colonists suffered at the hands of high-handed leaders.

2. Reasons why early English and French settlers concentrated on tobacco cultivation

The West Indies could and did produce a variety of tropical plants and crops. When one considers the reasons why emphasis was first placed on the cultivation of tobacco, however, one has to distinguish between food crops and crops that could be grown in commercial quantities.

Foodstuffs such as fruits and vegetables were of a perishable nature, that is, once ripe they could not remain sound for any appreciable length of time. The slowness and irregularity of the transatlantic crossing by sailing ships, which would have resulted in spoilage, therefore discouraged the production of these commodities for trade. Besides, fruits and vegetables were grown only to sustain life until supplies arrived from Europe. Their doubtful profitability, even if they could have been marketed abroad, discouraged their cultivation on a large scale.

Among the commodities which could be produced in commercial quantities in the climatic and soil conditions of the West Indies, were coffee, cotton, cocoa, corn, dyes and dye-woods, timber of various kinds, sugar and tobacco. Cattle could also be reared in the West Indies. The production of some of these commodities could be ruled out at once. The small ships of the 17th century could not profitably transport relatively bulky cargoes such as timber and cattle. Besides, to colonists seeking maximum profits, it would have served their purpose very little to have concentrated on the production of relatively cheap goods such as corn.

Early 17th century Europe was still seeking highly-prized essential or luxury goods for which Europeans had gone overseas in the 15th and 16th centuries. As far as they came from the West Indies, they included cocoa, coffee, sugar, cotton, dyes and tobacco. As beverages, cocoa and coffee were becoming increasingly popular but soon faced competition from tea from the East Indies. Sugar was used to sweeten these drinks but was as yet a comparatively expensive alternative to honey. Cotton and dyes could be sold but their market was restricted to cloth producers. Even so, the demand was small until the inventions of the Industrial Revolution in Britain during the second half of the 18th century promoted the production of textiles.

West Indian colonists produced a wide variety of goods, but the cultivation of tobacco occupied pride of place. Only tobacco, for a short period in the 17th century, satisfied all the conditions necessary for large-scale production. The smoking of tobacco or the taking of snuff was becoming fashionable or habitual in Europe and so created a ready market for the product. Tobacco clearly produced the greatest profit of all the commodities that could be produced. Once properly cured, tobacco was not perishable, nor was it so bulky as to pose major problems of transportation from the West Indies to Europe.

Tobacco had the added advantage of being relatively easy to cultivate. Tobacco could be grown on small plots which could be worked by a proprietor and his family together with a few extra hands; it did not require the large labour force necessary, for instance, in the cultivation of sugar. Besides, the processes involved in the preservation or curing of tobacco were relatively simple and did not call for large capital expenditure for the purchase of heavy machinery, buildings and livestock.

3. Changeover from tobacco to sugar. The part played by the Dutch

Throughout the West Indies, during the early years of settlement, tobacco had constituted the primary agricultural crop. Where sugar was planted at all in the Spanish islands, it was in insignificant and declining quantities. By the early 1640's it was introduced into the British Leeward Islands and thereafter its cultivation spread rapidly. Sugar production soon became more important than tobacco production. Several factors accounted for the changeover from tobacco to sugar-cane cultivation.

The relative profitability of crops that could be grown in the tropics decided their cultivation in the West Indies. By the mid-17th century, West Indian tobacco could compete neither in quantity nor in quality with that of the American colony of Virginia. Moreover, the combination of West Indian and Virginian tobacco created a glut in the European market which adversely affected prices and profits. A crop of greater profitability had to be found. The answer was sugar-cane.

Like tobacco, sugar-cane was a tropical product and could not be grown with success in the temperate climate of Europe. Europe, in any case, had not yet discovered the potential of sugar-beet. As in the case of tobacco also, the West Indies were suitable both in climate and in soil for the cultivation of sugar-cane. On geographical grounds, therefore, there was nothing to prevent the changeover from tobacco to sugar-cane. Like tobacco, again, the production of sugar posed no special transportation problems; sugar was not too bulky a commodity to be transported economically in the small ships then available. The essential requirements were the availability of suitable markets and the right prices. In these respects, conditions in Europe in the 17th century favoured the production of West Indian sugar.

Social habits in Europe at the time were changing. The introduction of tea and coffee into Europe from the newly-discovered lands overseas had resulted in the greater use there of these beverages. At the same time, in order to meet the ever-increasing demand, something less expensive than honey was needed to sweeten the new drinks. Attention was directed to cane sugar and the increased demand for this commodity provided a stimulus for its introduction and expansion in the West Indies. The English and French colonists readily accepted it as an alternative crop to tobacco and their efforts were supported by the Dutch.

Among the non-Hispanic European nations, the Dutch had already established their trading supremacy in the West Indies by the early 17th century. This supremacy was expressed in such a trading venture as the Dutch West India Company, formed in 1621, which established trading posts at strategic points throughout the Caribbean to exploit existent trading advantages. Settlements and colonies were founded for the same purpose, and not as plantation colonies. It was in connection with one of these that the Dutch became interested in West Indian sugar-cane cultivation. Around 1640, the Dutch were expelled from their settlement of Pernambuco in Brazil by the Portuguese. This expulsion represented considerable economic loss in planting and trade. As compensation, the Dutch decided to promote English and French enterprise in their plantation colonies. At Dutch instigation sugar was introduced, and Dutch advice helped to develop it. Assistance did not end there. The production of sugar required expensive capital equipment and this the Dutch helped to provide by supplying the necessary credit. Finally, the Dutch bought the planters' produce when the sugar was manufactured and provided a ready market for the young industry.

4. Consequences of large-scale sugar production in the West Indies

The effects of the change from tobacco to sugar in the West Indies have been termed the 'sugar revolution'. The changes were both rapid and far-reaching. They profoundly affected the economic conditions, the social structure and the political organisation of the islands.

The processing of sugar-cane into sugar required expensive buildings, livestock and machinery and for these to be economically worked meant that large quantities of cane had to be obtained. Factories could not be kept idle. Previously tobacco had been cultivated on relatively small plots; these were too small for the production of sugar-cane in economic quantities. Where it was not possible to acquire large enough holdings to cultivate sugar-cane, a process of absorption occurred to increase the size of existing estates. Small estates adjacent to larger ones were acquired, by fair means or foul, and wealthy and progressive planters took over the lands of their poorer or more backward neighbours. The net result was a reduction in the number of estates in any particular colony. As sugar became more profitable and as the demand for land, already in limited supply, increased, so did the price of land rise.

The change to sugar affected the racial composition of the colonies. The dispossession of small proprietors meant that a large number of people were forced to change their means of livelihood. Few, if any, of these people stayed to work for wages on the sugar plantations. Some drifted into urban occupations as inn-keepers, clerks and skilled craftsmen. Some emigrated to seek new fortunes in other colonies in the West Indies or in North America. Others took to the sea either as fishermen or as buccaneers. The flow of indentured white servants who had previously been attracted to the West Indies in the hope of becoming proprietors when their indenture ended, soon ceased as the incentive was removed. Efforts to provide a temporary labour force of Europeans through coercive methods such as kidnapping and forced transportation, or through bribery, propaganda, and recruitment through the courts, all failed.

Sugar cultivation, however, required a large disciplined labour force. With the failure of voluntary and compulsory emigration of Europeans to produce sufficient labourers to suit West Indian demands, the importation of negroes from Africa began. These people were not brought as indentures to labour for fixed periods, but as slaves subjected to compulsory labour throughout their entire lives. The number of these negroes increased rapidly. In Barbados, for example, there were only a few hundred slaves in 1640, but by 1645 there were over 6,000, and in 1685 there were over 46,000. While the negro population of the West Indies increased, the white population decreased. In Barbados, there were about 40,000 whites in 1645 but by 1685 these had decreased to about 20,000. By the end of the 17th century, negroes constituted the great majority of the population of both British and French islands. Attempts to maintain a certain proportion of whites to negroes by means of Deficiency Laws failed. Planters found it easier to pay the fines for breaches of the law than to secure the required number of whites.

The changed ethnic composition of the West Indies led inevitably to a changed social system. The introduction of so many negroes to the West Indies modified and shaped the character and habits of both whites and negroes. Social status came to be dominated by colour rather than as hitherto by purely economic achievement. The numerical difference between whites and negroes and the desire of the former to maintain their superiority meant that society came to be ordered by a policy of deliberate suppression of the dignity of the negroes by repressive legislation.

The cultivation of sugar increased the wealth to be obtained from the West Indies. This resulted in a change in the system of governing the colonies. Previously, the islands had been neglected by the crowns of the imperial powers, and as in the case of the British colonies, control was delegated to Lords-Proprietors. Their show of wealth and the financial gains to be derived from their control, however, showed the wisdom of bringing the islands under more direct crown control. From around 1660 the Lords-Proprietors were deprived of their authority and royal governors were sent out by the crown to govern the islands under more specific instructions and commissions. The proprietary system of government gave way to the representative system (representative albeit of a very restricted section of the population).

Certain other changes of a combined economic and political nature were introduced with the advent of sugar-cane. The Navigation Acts of the 1650's and 1660's sought to end Dutch trading supremacy in the West Indies and to reserve the trade for Britain. The Acts aimed to draw closer the political bonds of empire by bringing the islands further under royal government in the process of greater centralisation. Similar laws were passed by France in the 1670's.

The increasing wealth of the West Indies due to the introduction and expansion of sugar-cane, aroused the greed of European nations who sought to wrest control of the islands from each other. There were West Indian ambitions in each European war, and war in Europe was accompanied by war in the West Indies. The late 17th century and the whole of the 18th century witnessed the shuffling, backward and forward, of the islands from one European nation to another, as the fortunes of war changed. The West Indies thus became pawns in the game of international politics, and the region became a theatre of maritime warfare.

5. The layout and organisation of an ordinary West Indian sugar plantation

West Indian sugar estates varied in size from a few hundred to several thousand acres, according to soil, climatic and physical geographical conditions. An average estate measured about five hundred acres and was laid out according to an almost regular pattern.

The estate land consisted of a number of clearly defined parts. In the hey-day of plantation agriculture, the greater part of the estate was devoted to sugar-cane cultivation. This portion was usually the best land since the planter's aim was maximum profit which could be secured from soil utilisation. Sugar-cane land was usually divided into sections or fields in order to facilitate land use, that is, one part could be planted while another was reaped.

A part of the estate was also used as provision grounds for the production of such food as root-crops and vegetables to feed the large numbers of estate slaves. As sugar-cane production expanded in response to increasing demand for sugar, and in view of the limited size of estates, this part tended to decrease in size and to be confined to the less productive parts of the estates. These were mostly rocky slopes and foothills of mountains, and other marginal or sub-marginal sugar producing areas.

A third portion of the estate was devoted to woodlands where the estate supply of construction timber, logs and firewood was obtained. Wattles and thatch for slave dwellings were also obtained here. As time passed, this section of the estate also tended to decrease, the estate requirements being met by imports. Each estate devoted a part of its lands to the pasturing of livestock, primarily cattle, horses and mules which were used either as draft animals or to supply manure.

Though primarily devoted to sugar-cane cultivation, an estate was not exclusively devoted to this. Other commercial crops such as tobacco, cotton, pimento, ginger and indigo were also grown for export. These crops occupied only a small portion of the estate.

In addition to its agricultural crops, each estate had its own buildings and works. There were, for instance, the mills for crushing the canes, the boiling-house, the curing-house, and, if rum was distilled, the still-house. There were workshops for skilled wheelwrights, carpenters, coopers, blacksmiths and masons. In addition, there was usually a hospital for the sick and a small gaol for slaves in punishment. Sheds were constructed for livestock and to store bagasse. And store-rooms were built to keep produce and equipment.

THE PLAN OF A SUGAR ESTATE

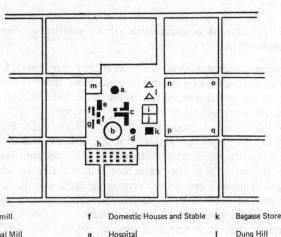

a	Windmill	f	Domestic Houses and Stable	k	Bagasse Store
b	Animal Mill	g	Hospital	l	Dung Hill
c	Boiling House	h	Slave Cottages	m	Kitchen Garden
d	Well	i	Cattle Pen	n o p q	Sugar Cane Field
e	Dwelling House	j	Donkey Stable and Pen		

Near the factory buildings were the houses occupied by the estate manager, overseers and book-keepers. The estate owner or his attorney, if resident, usually lived apart in grander style in the estate's 'Great House'.

The slave quarters were set apart from the residences of the whites. Their living quarters might be small huts for individual families, or large barracks divided into compartments to house several families. Attached to these were very small plots to be used as gardens where slaves might grow supplementary food supplies.

6. The cultivation of sugar-cane and the manufacture of sugar

Before sugar-cane was cultivated the land had to be prepared. The ground had to be cleared of bush, shrubs and grass, and where necessary, drainage and irrigation canals dug. On hillsides, in order to prevent soil erosion, it was sometimes necessary to terrace the land before cultivation. The ground was then marked off for tilling.

Because ploughs were not introduced until late during slavery, if at all, tilling was done by slaves with heavy digging hoes, in a process called 'holing'. Holes were dug about four feet square and from six to nine inches deep. Into each hole some animal manure was dumped and cane cuttings or 'tops' were laid at the bottom and lightly covered over with soil. Rows were usually parallel to each other. Planting was usually done just before the start of a rainy season. While the cuttings grew, they were 'moulded' by refilling the holes with the soil originally removed.

Planting in the same field was done only periodically since, after the first year, the canes were allowed to grow from the portion of stem which was left after the cane was reaped. This process was known as ratoon cultivation and might be allowed for five to seven or more years depending on the fertility of the soil.

While the sugar-cane was growing, the rows were kept free of weeds which would hamper its growth. Three or more weedings were usually done. As the sugar-cane grew bigger, weeding became less necessary since less sunlight penetrated to the ground to nourish the weeds there.

In twelve to fifteen months, the crop was ready for reaping. Usually the canes which grew from ratoons ripened earlier than those which grew from tops. Cutting was done by slaves using cutlasses or machetes. Cut canes were tied into bundles and transported to the factories in carts.

At the factory, the canes were passed through the mills consisting of a number of rotating iron rollers. The juice, or liquor, was extracted and conveyed by gutters into receptacles called siphons. The cane trash or 'bagasse' was collected, dried and used as fuel under the various boilers. In the siphons the juice was clarified by heating and the addition of a small amount of lime. The impurities were skimmed off and later used with molasses in the distillation of rum. From the siphons the liquor was transferred to the first and largest of three boilers or 'coppers' where it was boiled for some time. After a certain amount of evaporation had taken place, the contents were emptied into a second and smaller copper where boiling continued but at a higher temperature. After more condensation had taken place, the liquid was transferred to the last and smallest copper. Here it was heated until it became so thick that a drop would stretch between one's fingers. This sticky substance was called teaché.

The teaché was emptied into large shallow coolers where it remained until it was almost cold. It was then put into hogsheads with perforated bottoms, which were placed on sloping platforms in the curing-house. There they remained for about three weeks during which the molasses dripped out leaving the sugar crystals in the hogsheads. These were then sealed and sent off to be shipped to their European or American market.

7. Reasons for planters' dissatisfaction and grievances in the 18th century

Economic

(i) The 18th century was a period of almost incessant warfare among European nations interspersed with periods of uneasy peace. The West Indies became involved as colonies of participating nations. The War of Spanish Succession extended from 1702 to 1713; the War of Jenkin's Ear and the War of the Austrian Succession lasted from 1739 to 1748; the Seven Years' War from 1756 to 1763; the War of American Independence from 1776 to 1783; and the French Revolutionary and Napoleonic Wars from 1793 to 1815. War disrupted trade while enemy attack, destruction and conquest prevented continuous economic development.

(ii) War made it difficult to procure adequate supplies and, as in the case of the American War, severed established channels of trade to the disadvantage of the British islands.

(iii) The prices of West Indian staple products rose steadily during the war periods, but profit benefits to planters were largely negated by increased production, transportation and marketing costs.

(iv) The cost of installing capital equipment for the production of sugar was always costly and increased with the uncertainties of war.

(v) Though weakened somewhat by the establishment of free ports in certain selected islands like Jamaica, Dominica, Grenada, the Bahamas, Antigua and Trinidad, the Navigation Acts imposed severe restrictions on British West Indian freedom of trade.

(vi) The curtailments of war and the restrictions of trade made it difficult to maintain adequate supplies of slaves to work the plantations and to make adequate provision for their upkeep especially in times of drought or hurricane.

(vii) The plantation system operated on loans obtainable in Britain. The interest rates on these loans were high and imposed grave hardships. Efforts made by West Indians to secure a reduction of these rates proved unavailing.

Social

(i) Life in the West Indies was marred by the lack of adequate educational facilities, medical care, poor relief, police and prison services, religious instruction and religious services. In many instances these social services were lacking completely, or where existing were haphazardly conducted.

(ii) To colonists a colony was important according to the quantity of wealth that could be extracted from it. Little effort was made to provide such amenities as roads, and bad or impassable roads made transportation and communication difficult.

(iii) West Indian society was a slave society, that is, it required the labour of slaves to work the plantations. Maximum performance by slaves necessitated coercion, and coercion in the form of flogging, torture and dismemberment, together with the slaves' will to be free, evoked retaliation among the slaves. The white community lived in constant fear of slave rebellion or uprising.

(iv) The dominant fears among white colonists were of violence by the slaves and economic competition by the free-negroes and coloureds. The desire to maintain their superior status in society, and at the same time secure the subordination of the lower classes, forced the whites to devise ways and means, expressed in restrictive legislation, to order the relationship among the various social classes.

(v) Despite the apparent solidarity among the whites in view of the opposition, anticipated and real, from the lower classes, they were not a unified group. Their own differences bred fear and the smaller planters were always afraid of being bought out by more powerful planters. With the expansion of sugar cultivation in the 18th century, many small estates devoted to tobacco and cotton situated near sugar plantations were purchased and their owners forced to change occupation.

Political

 (i) The white colonists always found it necessary to satisfy certain property and sometimes residential qualifications before they could participate as candidates and electors during elections for the local House of Assembly. Freedom to participate was not automatic. Nomination to the Council was even more restricted since this was reserved for the most wealthy or influential planters, merchants or government officials.

 (ii) Prosperity bred absentee landlordism, and absenteeism bred corresponding problems. It became more difficult to secure the best qualified people to fill political positions and this reduced the quality of government. Those who left the West Indies were not replaced by new colonists; the result was a smaller ratio of whites to negroes, a factor which encouraged negro resistance.

(iii) Constant differences over rights and privileges between the councils and assemblies fostered political instability and an atmosphere of insecurity which the whites found irksome.

(iv) Despite the apparent freedom to legislate which British West Indian legislatures possessed, they nevertheless occupied a subordinate position to the British parliament. For instance, all colonial acts were subject to the approval of the crown, while the British Government reserved the right to intervene in local affairs. West Indians often found their subordinate position very frustrating.

8. Causes for the decline of British plantation agriculture

(*a*) Absenteeism: this bred lack of incentive and gave rise to dishonesty by attorneys and managers motivated bv the need for personal gain.

(*b*) The operations of a restrictive trade policy: the British West Indies could not legally take advantage of other more profitable markets than Britain.

(*c*) The independence of the American colonies: after independence the British West Indies could no longer legally buy from or sell to them since they had acquired the status of a foreign country. Thus the colonies were deprived of one of their best markets. The purchase of essential foodstuff, lumber and animals for use by the estates, and the sale of estate produce (principally sugar and molasses), were restricted.

(*d*) The abolition of the slave trade in 1807: this increased the cost of production since planters had to breed slaves and to provide them with better amenities.

(*e*) Development of the beet sugar industry in Europe: this resulted in increasing competition against British West Indian sugar re-exported from Britain.

(*f*) Shortage of credit money to transact the business of estates and to effect improvements. Even when credit was received, it carried a high interest rate.

(*g*) Natural disasters, for example, hurricane in the British Virgin Islands in 1819. These disasters destroyed the credit-value of many estates and forced them out of production.

(*h*) Destructions and dislocations caused by the French Revolutionary and Napoleonic Wars: these weakened the powers of recovery of many planters.

(*i*) Lower prices for British West Indian sugar in Europe because of competition from Cuban, Brazilian and East Indian sugar. After 1815 also, France was supplied by its own colonies, and the American demand was partly met from Louisiana, thereby reducing dependence on the British West Indies.

(*j*) Increased marketing and production costs of estate produce.

(*k*) Britain was industrialising and concentrating its financial resources in industry and could not give required financial assistance to the colonies. Requests for aid (loans and grants) were usually disregarded or refused.

(*l*) Lower fertility of soils due to overworking, and failure of planters to use fertilisers: this resulted in lower yields.

(*m*) Heavy taxation on sugar (by way of duties) as compared with that on other estate or colonial produce.

(*n*) Inefficient machinery led to wasteage in the process of manufacturing sugar-cane into sugar. Only a relatively small fraction of the sugar in canes was usually extracted.

(*o*) Failure of planters to introduce labour-saving devices, for example, ploughs and harrows, and their reliance on slave labour which was wasteful, inefficient and non-economic.

9. The West India Interest

A marked feature of British West Indian history was the existence of absentee landlordism, that is, the habit of owners of West Indian plantations to leave control to attorneys and managers and reside away from their estates. Many of these planters lived in Britain after acquiring large sums of money in the West Indies. In addition, many individuals in Britain who had never lived in the West Indies rose to wealth by inheriting West Indian plantations. The numerical strength of the absentee planters was increased by the large number of West Indian merchants in Britain who drew huge profits from trade with the West Indies. To these can be added the colonial agents and factors. The factors were responsible for the sale of estate produce and for the purchase and despatch of estate supplies, while the colonial agents represented the interest of the colonies to officials and other authorities in Britain. The combination of absentee planters, merchants, colonial agents and factors is usually referred to as 'the West India Interest'. Their solidarity was expressed in such organisations as the Society of West India Planters and Merchants of London formed in the 1760's.

Because of the great wealth of the West India Interest, its influence was considerable. Planters and merchants not only purchased immense property in Britain, but they rivalled the aristocracy in splendid ostentatious living. Their influence also extended to the sphere of politics. The British political climate in the 18th and early 19th centuries favoured them. As Dr. Eric Williams has pointed out, 'In the classic age of parliamentary corruption and electoral venality their money talked. They bought votes and rotten boroughs and so got into Parliament'. Members of the West India Interest entrenched themselves not only in the House of Commons but also in the House of Lords. It was not until 1832 by the reform of Parliament that their political power was reduced. Political gains were used to advance West Indian interests, namely, the defence of plantation agriculture and the social structure which it promoted.

The efforts of the West India Interest were not always successful, but their influence was sometimes considerable. This was due to their alliance with the landed aristocracy and commercial middle-class (who were also monopolists). The activities of the West India Interest probably had some influence on the British decision to restore the islands of Guadeloupe and Martinique to France in 1763 (at the close of the Seven Years' War) in return for Canada, since the sugar from these islands could compete dangerously with the product from the

British islands if they remained within the Empire. The West India Interest was also instrumental in securing the passage by Parliament of the Sugar Act of 1764 which was designed to eliminate trading between the American colonies and the foreign West Indies. In this way they sought a wider market for their own product. Their attempt failed to produce any benefits—the only notable result was the stimulus which they gave to the cause of independence in the American colonies. After the Declaration of American Independence, the West India Interest fought, again unsuccessfully, to secure the continuation of trading privileges between the British West Indies and the United States. They opposed attempts to increase duties on sugar and resisted any attempt to curtail their monopoly. Their greatest rearguard actions were taken with reference to the abolition of the slave trade and to the emancipation of slaves. Propaganda pamphlets and lectures outside Parliament supplemented efforts to exert pressure within Parliament for the preservation of these institutions.

In the 19th century, the influence of the West India Interest waned. Part of the explanation lay in the fact of economic decline of the British West Indies. The reduced profitability of West Indian agriculture reduced the means of the interest to conduct campaigns of resistance. In the 18th century the West India Interest had operated with the assistance of powerful friends. But by the 19th century the planters' recalcitrance and their wilful refusal to grant concessions to the anti-slavery sentiment in Britain, alienated these friends. At the same time, those who were opposed to the West India Interest became correspondingly stronger. The early 19th century was one of enlightened reform spurred by the upsurge of religious sentiment and the spirit of *laissez faire*. Those who, like the West India Interest, practised, encouraged, or sought to promote oppression, and who adhered to monopolistic practices, were doomed to failure.

Conclusion

The main attraction of the West Indies to European settlers was the wealth to be obtained in the region. Some settlers came of their own accord to escape an uncertain future in Europe and to build a better life. Others were forced to come as transportees. All suffered from an unfavourable West Indian climate and geography, tropical diseases, inadequate social services, scarcity of supplies, attacks from Caribs and from other European colonising powers, and poor administration.

The West Indies could grow a variety of tropical crops. At first the emphasis was on tobacco and later on sugar-cane cultivation. Both crops were in demand in Europe and could therefore be grown profitably. The possibility of easy and safe transportation to Europe was also important. The change-over from tobacco to sugar-cane was revolutionary—it affected the social, economic and political conditions of the West Indies. Socially it led to the introduction of negro slaves in greater numbers than the white population and led to the emergence of a society of various classes. Economically, it led to the emergence of the large plantation and an almost complete dependence upon sugar, and the adoption of restrictive navigation laws by imperial powers. Politically, it led to more centralised control by the mother-country of the respective colonies, and promoted international rivalry and war.

The subordination of West Indian colonies to their 'home' countries caused several hardships to the colonists, especially with regard to freedom of trade and the exercise of political power. Restrictive trade laws undoubtedly contributed to West Indian economic decline. Absentee-ownership, competition from European beet-sugar and from cane-sugar from Cuba, Brazil and the East Indies, lack of finances by planters, and the exhaustion of West Indian soils, underlined the decline of British as well as French West Indian plantation agriculture. Against these disadvantages the West India Interest fought a losing battle.

Plantation agriculture could not be undertaken without an adequate labour force. When tobacco cultivation gave way to sugar-cane, a large labour force became a necessity. This was provided by negroes from Africa. But labour did not only have to be plentiful, it also had to be economical or cheap. To planters, greater economy could be achieved by employing the Africans as slaves. The concomitant of the plantation system was negro slavery.

Revision Questions

1. What commodities did the West Indies produce in the early years of their settlement?
2. What problems were likely to face the early English and French settlers?
3. Why was there emphasis on one or two main crops in the West Indies?
4. Why was the cultivation of sugar-cane on a large scale considered revolutionary?
5. What is usually understood by the terms cane land, provision ground and woodland? Describe the part played by each on a sugar estate.
6. What difficulties were experienced by a West Indian planter?

3. Slavery

The change from small-scale to large-scale agriculture in the West Indies was accompanied by a change in the system of recruiting labour. Until the introduction of sugar cultivation for export purposes, the demand for labour had been almost adequately met by indentured European servants. Plantation agriculture demanded a larger labour force than was hitherto available or was henceforth possible to obtain. European indentures were not willing to come to the West Indies in anything like the required numbers and the answer to the labour problem was found in the importation of negro slaves from Africa who possessed the essential qualities for work on the plantations.

The profits from the trade in African slaves attracted many dealers of all nations who were prepared to operate both legally and illegally. For more than two centuries, the Atlantic between the West Indies and West Africa, the 'Middle Passage' of a triangular trade route having as its points Europe, Africa, and the Caribbean, was thronged by these slave traders. From being at first a Portuguese monopoly because of the monopoly over colonial Africa and Africans which Portugal possessed as a result of the Pope's grant in the 1490's, the slave trade attracted other maritime European nations, for example, England, France, the Netherlands, Sweden and Denmark. The challenge and infringement of Spanish monopoly in the West Indies was accompanied by a similar challenge to Portuguese monopoly in Africa. The two were closely inter-related. From being at first the unco-ordinated activity of individual traders of the various European nations, the slave trade came to be dominated by organised national companies.

Conditions under which slaves were recruited in West Africa and then shipped to the West Indies, were not much different in character from the conditions under which they existed on the sugar plantations. Recruitment promoted inter-tribal jealousy, strife and war among Africans encouraged by profit-seeking Europeans. The brutal ruthlessness of the inhuman traffic in human beings was symbolised by the slave forts and factories with their inevitable barracoons. Here Africans were converted by sale into slaves destined to labour on West Indian plantations. The misery in Africa was continued in the Atlantic crossing where fear of the unknown, death by disease on overcrowded slave ships, and continuous attempts at suicide were among the most outstanding features. For the survivors, a new life as plantation labourers awaited them. On the estates, life was a prolonged degradation interspersed by attempts to escape or resist. The revolution in St. Domingue in 1791, and the establishment of the negro republic of Haiti was merely an extreme example of the attempt made by enslaved people to escape their lot and assert their human dignity and worth.

Conditions under which slaves lived and worked were harsh. They laboured unremittingly with inadequate food, clothing, housing and medical care, and with severe restrictions placed on their freedom of movement.

Slavery led to the development in the West Indies of a society classified according to colour, wealth and education. Slaves automatically reverted to the bottom of the social hierarchy and their inferior position was written into discriminatory legislation. So too, but to a less extent, was that of the free negroes and free-coloureds who occupied a middle social position. The whites formed the highest class by reason of their colour, and their economic and political privileges.

At an early stage, the servile condition under which slaves existed, attracted the attention of various groups of humanitarians in Europe who agitated for an end to both the slave trade and slavery. The debates between the supporters and opponents of slavery were long and bitter. In effect, their arguments represented not only conflict between good and evil but also between monopoly and laissez faire since the fight against slavery was only one aspect of the struggle for social, economic and political freedom being currently waged in Europe. In England, the victory of the opponents of slavery was marked by the abolition of the slave trade in 1808 and, after a vain attempt to secure the improvement of harsh slave conditions, by the emancipation of slaves in 1834.

1. The types of labourers used in the West Indies before 1838

The earliest European colonists in the West Indies certainly did much of their own labour. The types of occupations in which they engaged facilitated self-employment. For example, cattle rearing which was a primary pursuit of Spaniards in the West Indies, as in Spain, did not require much labour. Similarly, tobacco cultivation by the early English and French colonists, could be done by the settler family and a few assistants. Many early colonists, too, could not afford the economic upkeep of hired labour. But whenever and wherever possible, Europeans sought the labour of others to assist them. As time went on and as the Europeans became wealthier, they became involved in labour-intensive industries such as sugar production. They began to consider physical labour beneath the dignity of white men and depended more and more on others. These factors determined the types of labourers used in the West Indies between 1492 and 1838.

Among the first people who assisted the European colonists were the native Indians. These Indians, in the West Indies, were primarily of Arawak stock, the Caribs proving too hostile to be subjected. The natives were subjected to forced labour and were made to work in the gold and silver mines and on cattle ranches. These occupations, however, were alien to their nature and sometimes beyond their physical strength. Overwork and ill-treatment contributed to the depletion of the native population which was largely due to diseases introduced by Europeans.

The first protest against Indian exploitation was made by a Dominican friar named Montesinos in 1511. He spoke from the pulpit, sometimes to the chagrin of his congregation, and he presented his case to the Spanish king in person. Montesinos, however, was overshadowed by Las Casas who made himself a spokesman for those working for Indian rights. In 1516 Las Casas was made Protector of the Indians and he devoted his life to the cause of Indian liberty. To Las Casas is sometimes attributed the idea of substituting African slave labour for that of Indians. This is not supported by evidence. Be that as it may, when the native Indians proved to be unsatisfactory labourers, recourse was had to the labour of negroes. The first negroes who came to the West Indies were brought from Spain. The negroes were used as slaves and as the demand for them increased they were brought direct from Africa. The English, French and other non-Spanish European colonists followed the example of the Spaniards. With the introduction of sugar-cane to replace tobacco in the West Indies and the demand for a large labour force, a considerable trade in Africans was opened.

Throughout the West Indies, African negroes were employed as slaves. They were the main source of labour supply in the West Indies and eventually came to be the only one. Even before this happened, however, an attempt had been made to recruit European indentured labourers to perform field labour. The attempt met with varying degrees of success. While the West Indies possessed the status of a frontier region, and while large tracts of land were available for distribution, European indentures were relatively easy to attract. After their period of indenture ended, which was usually after five years, the labourers could move on to make their fortunes elsewhere in the Caribbean or remain in the islands where they could occupy land and plant for themselves. Later, when all available land in the West Indies, or rather the best cultivable portions, had been occupied, especially after the introduction of sugar-cane, the incentive for European indentures was removed. Then, too, the cultivation of sugar-cane forced many small planters out of production since their estates or plots were absorbed by the large sugar planters. Again, in order to maintain a balance between the whites and negroes in the West Indies, Deficiency Laws were passed in order to maintain the numbers of whites. Because or in spite of the various factors involved, it was difficult to secure European labourers for the West Indies despite attempts to do so by means of forced methods such as crimping and kidnapping.

Until, 1838, European labour continued to be applied to economic production in the West Indies but in a manner different from the early years of colonisation. While negro slaves contributed their physical labour to plantation agriculture, the direction and initiative for improvement and expansion were given by the whites who controlled the economy. Both were essential factors in the production of West Indian commodities.

2. Participants in the African slave trade

All maritime European nations which held colonies in the West Indies participated in the African slave trade at one time or another.

The Spaniards were the first to enter and settle in the West Indies, and they were the first to use negroes as labourers when the supply of labour from the native Indians failed them. In 1502, the first negro slaves were brought over from Spain where considerable numbers had already been employed for some time before. As the demand for negro labour increased, however, supplies were obtained direct from Africa.

In 1517, the Spanish king granted a licence to one of his favourite courtiers, Laurent de Gouvenot, to supply African slaves to the American colonies. De Gouvenot disposed of his privilege to various slave-trading merchants. These obtained their slaves from Portuguese dealers who alone, at the time, were allowed to visit the African coast because of Pope Alexander's bulls giving Portugal legal claim to all lands east of the line of demarcation.

When de Gouvenot's licence expired in 1538, the king sold the exclusive right to supply slaves to the West Indian colonies to two German merchants. This was the beginning of the 'asiento'.

The 4,000 slaves that could be transported to America every year were insufficient to meet the demand there. Prices were inevitably high. These two factors of short supply and high prices led to an illicit traffic in slaves by European interlopers. Spanish colonists were willing to buy from foreigners despite the stringent Spanish laws against such trade. Facility for smuggling was given by the long stretches of unguarded coastlines and sometimes by accommodating Spanish officials.

The first interlopers were the Portuguese who, under the pretence that they were providing their Brazilian colony with slaves, in fact supplied the Spanish colonies. The Portuguese were later joined by English and Dutch interlopers. Even Spaniards who had failed to secure the necessary licence to participate in the slave trade, engaged in the illegal traffic. The long African coastline which the Portuguese could not adequately defend, made the recruitment of slaves possible. The interlopers sold their cargoes comparatively cheaply and they became popular with the colonists especially as they were willing to take payment for their slaves in pearl, cattle hides and sugar, which made the trade easier for the colonists than if cash had been demanded.

When the English and French established their West Indian colonies in the first half of the 17th century, they supplied their own African slaves. But the demand was small since settlers were largely content to work in the fields they owned and to hire other white men to work for them. King James I issued the first exclusive slave charter to Englishmen in 1618. The Company failed and a new enterprise was sanctioned by Charles I in 1631. This proved adequate to meet the meagre demands of the time.

The labour situation changed with the introduction of large-scale sugar-cane cultivation after the 1640's. There was a demand for slaves in large numbers. At about the same time the Dutch captured the Portuguese establishments in Africa and so came to exercise a virtual monopoly over the slave trade. Their trading position was strengthened since they were able to provide West Indian sugar-cane planters with the credit necessary to buy slaves.

The Dutch did not hold their monopoly for long. The large profits to be made from the slave trade made European nations which had plantation colonies provide their own slaves and engage in interloping wherever possible. Individual traders trading on their own account gave way to organised national companies in the second half of the 17th century since it was expensive to maintain slave-trading establishments in Africa. England, France, Sweden, Denmark and Brandenburgh all had such companies. Not all of these were successful and they were sooner or later replaced by private traders.

Among the most successful companies was the British Royal

African Company which was formed in 1672 with a monopoly of the slave trade to the English colonies. Complaints against the Company of high prices and of irregular and insufficient supplies of slaves, led to the slave trade being thrown open to all traders in 1689, subject to only the payment of dues to the Company which was still responsible for the maintenance of the English establishments in West Africa. This arrangement lasted until 1714 when the 'asiento', or the right to sell slaves to the Spanish colonies, was awarded to the British by the Treaty of Utrecht. It became the monopoly of the South Sea Company to which private traders and the Royal African Company could sell slaves. The Treaty of Aix-la-Chapelle in 1748 confirmed the British right to the 'asiento', but neither Britain nor Spain was anxious for it to continue, and by a commercial treaty in 1750, all claims to the 'asiento' were surrendered by Britain in return for a payment of £100,000 by Spain. When this was done, the activities of the South Sea Company ceased and the slave trade was carried on by small independent concerns. Illicit trade in slaves with the Spanish colonies continued on a reduced scale.

By the second half of the 18th century, until it was brought to an end by the respective European countries, individual traders dominated the slave trade. They had the blessings of the national governments.

3. Description of the slave trade as it occurred in Africa, the Middle Passage and the West Indies

The trade in Africa was organised around slaving forts established at strategic points along the West African coast. In charge of the forts were governors who were responsible for giving protection to slave dealers against 'external' European invasion, and 'internal' African attack. Agents or 'factors' were responsible for the purchase and sale of slaves. Priests often acted as intermediaries between agents and African suppliers of slaves. In addition, to the forts there were factories which were situated farther inland.

Recruitment of Africans during the early years of the trade took place relatively near the coast, that is, within a radius of about thirty miles from the fort, but as the demand increased, it was necessary to go farther inland sometimes as much as five to six hundred miles. Slaves consisted of criminals and prisoners of war. Petty wars between native tribes were encouraged to secure adequate numbers. Groups of Africans were herded to the coast under protection. At nights lodging was sought in friendly villages. Taxes were levied on slave bands by local chieftains in return for permission to pass through their territory. At the fort or factory, the Africans were lodged in barracoons where they awaited sale. The price of Africans went up

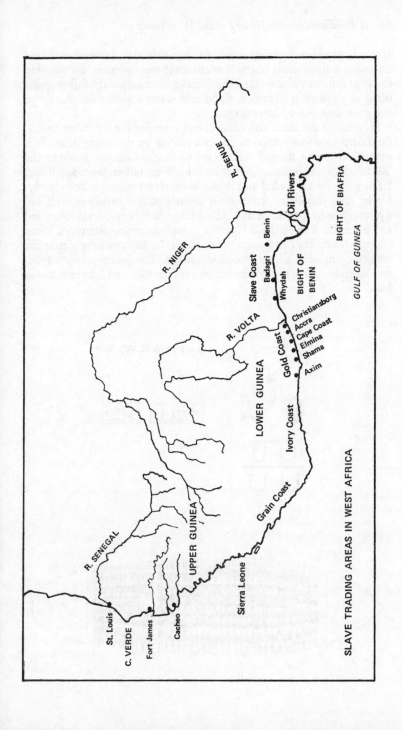

SLAVE TRADING AREAS IN WEST AFRICA

as the demand for slaves increased. After sale the slaves were transferred on board ship in small boats. Sometimes it was necessary for the ship to call at different points along the African coast before the full complement of slaves was obtained. Food and water supplies for the cargo and crew had also to be procured.

Escape was the main aim of all slaves intended for the West Indies. On board ship many tried to commit suicide by throwing themselves overboard. Some starved themselves to death. Conditions along the 'Middle Passage' between Africa and the West Indies, were appalling. Ships were overcrowded and in the holds slaves were packed closely. Under such conditions, contagious diseases such as smallpox, itch and dysentery were prevalent and killed large numbers. Slaves were fed and given exercise on deck. Doctors provided medical attention. Some captains were kind and some were harsh. In any case, the desire for profits dominated all other considerations. The journey lasted from five to eight weeks if the weather was favourable, and longer if it was bad.

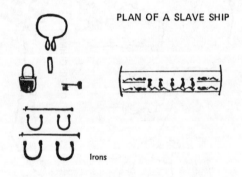

PLAN OF A SLAVE SHIP

Irons

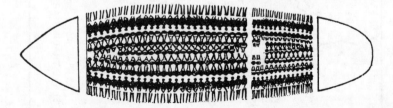

At the West Indian port, the slaves were sold on board ship or on the wharves. They were bathed, oiled and trimmed to show them to advantage. Advertisements in the local newspapers or on billboards giving the age, sex, and tribal origin of the slaves often preceded sale. Africans noted for docile and industrious qualities sold more easily and for higher prices than others that were thought to be war-like and not given to labour. Once bought, slaves were clothed and conducted to the plantations where they were put under the charge of experienced slaves who initiated them into the various aspects of plantation life and work. The length of the 'seasoning' period depended upon the immediate need of the plantation for labour.

4. Social grouping during slavery: group differences

While slavery existed, West Indian society was highly stratified, the stratification being based on a combination of colour, wealth and education. One alone was not enough. Only people who possessed these attributes in greatest measure were assured of a position at the top of the social ladder. Alternatively, those who possessed the least attributes were relegated to a position at the bottom. On the basis of these qualifications, three broad classes or divisions of people developed in the West Indies. At the top were the whites, while at the bottom was the mass of negro slaves. Between these two groups was a class of free negroes and coloureds. The free negroes originated from slaves who had purchased or had been given their freedom by their owners for faithful service, while the free coloureds originated as the children of masters and slaves. The numbers of both free negroes and coloureds increased as a result of the birth of children in both sections.

Within each of the main groups of people there was further subdivision. Among the whites, for instance, the large planters (or their attorneys and managers), merchants and professional people such as doctors and lawyers occupied a place at the top, followed by overseers, book-keepers, skilled artisans and small shopkeepers; at the bottom were the 'poor whites' who considered labour to be beneath their dignity. The slaves were also divided, in descending order of importance, into artisans, domestics and field-slaves. Sub-divisions were less noticeable among the free negroes and coloureds, but status was undoubtedly influenced by degrees of colour, wealth and education.

One class of people require special mention. This was the white missionary group. The white missionaries though educated were disqualified for a high position in the social hierarchy because of their lack of wealth. In any case, they were not considered a regular part of the white community. To some extent they preferred to occupy an independent position on the fringe of the white community in order to preserve their religious freedom and to avoid corruption. Their vocation made it necessary for them to establish that they served all classes and were subservient to none.

The whites occupied the dominant position in society. Only whites held the political franchise and occupied seats in the legislative assemblies. Membership of the councils was also reserved for the elite whites. There was no legal limit to the amount of land and number of slaves the whites desired and could afford to have. They had power to enact discriminatory legislation to control the lives and activities of the other two lower social groups and to establish and maintain their own superiority. Control of the legislature was accompanied by a similar control over the administration, both civil and judicial, and over the military. This meant that only whites held government offices, occupied positions as judges, magistrates, and justices of the peace, and were appointed as officers in the local militias. If the missionaries are to be included, then the whites also had control over the Church and its activities.

The free negroes and coloureds suffered from economic, social and political disabilities which were sanctioned by law. The amount of land and slaves which they could own was limited unless they were prepared to pay certain higher taxes on them. Their socially inferior position was expressed in many ways: they had to secure patrons from among the whites who would vouchsafe for them and speak on their behalf, and striking a white person irrespective of the latter's social status was a legal offence punishable by whipping, imprisonment and dismemberment. They could not participate in elections either as electors or candidates. They could not occupy administrative or judicial positions, and in the militia, though they could bear arms, they had to serve under white officers and receive smaller awards of compensation. In the later years of slavery many of the restrictions on the freedom of free negroes and coloureds were removed. By that time, many had advanced economically as a result of agricultural and business ventures.

The greatest disabilities were suffered by the slaves who performed the heavy manual work on the estates whether as artisans responsible for making carts and barrels, or for constructing buildings, or as domestics responsible for cooking, washing or sweeping, or as field slaves responsible for weeding, planting, reaping, digging or carting. The menial work in which they were engaged underlined their inferior social position. This was emphasised by the conditions under which they lived and worked. They were under the absolute control of their masters whose responsibilities towards them with regard to the provision of food, housing, clothes and medical care, were not always clearly defined. Severe restrictions were imposed on their economic opportunities. In keeping with their servile status, slaves could not themselves become owners or employers of slaves, or cultivate sugar-cane or other staple crops. Their agricultural opportunities were confined to the cultivation of small plots for food. Like the free negroes and coloureds, slaves were subject to severe penalties for striking a white person. In their case they could be executed. Slaves could not bear arms, and they could not freely leave the estate except to go to market; to go elsewhere required a pass from the owner. Nothing could better express the inferior position of slaves than the laws regulating funerals which stipulated that slaves could be buried only in plain deal board coffins. Slaves had no political rights throughout the entire period of slavery.

5. Living and working conditions of slaves on an estate

The essence of slavery was that the negro slaves were chattels dependent for their existence on the charity, generosity or beneficence of their masters who provided their daily sustenance. The care of the master extended to the provision of housing, food, clothing and medical care. In return, slaves were expected to labour continuously whether in the factory as artisans, in the master's house as domestics, or in the fields as labourers.

In contrast to the estate owner or his attorney who lived in the 'Great House', the slaves lived in huts or barracks built of timber, wattle and thatch. The walls were daubed with mud and the floor was invariably the bare earth. In odd cases, the lodging of the more well-to-do slaves had shingled roofs. Slave-quarters had little furniture, and beds were either laid on the ground or raised on wooden bunks. Overcrowding was common and this encouraged the spread of contagious diseases such as yaws, malaria, ringworm and itch.

The clothing and feeding of slaves was a major responsibility of their owners. Two units of clothes a year were the usual allowance. These were of a coarse linen—osnaburg, Dutch stripes or guinée bleue. Food was either imported, produced on a portion of the plantation, or was grown by the slaves on the small plots of land allocated to them. In most of the islands, as sugar cultivation expanded to include the estate provision grounds and even the slaves plots, more and more food was imported. In the larger islands, sugar-cane expansion drove the slaves to cultivate land of low productivity thereby creating dependence on imported foodstuffs. Dependence on imports often caused distress and sometimes widespread disaster when supplies were interrupted. The awareness of the danger of starvation such as in times of war, led to strenuous efforts to introduce new food plants into the West Indies. In 1778 the ackee was introduced from West Africa, and in 1793, the breadfruit was introduced from the Pacific island of Tahiti.

Medical care was also provided for the slaves. Many of the larger estates had resident doctors and hospitals to cater for the illness of slaves. Even where these facilities did not exist financial provision was made by the estate owner for the medical services of a visiting doctor.

While some attempt was made by the estate owners to provide their slaves with the basic necessities of life, education was neglected. To some extent planters saw no necessity for this, and to some extent they feared that education would give slaves notions of equality which would interfere with their performance as labourers, and which they might seek to achieve by violent means. Education was, therefore, discouraged, or, as in the case of religious instruction, encouraged to the extent which made slaves more amenable to discipline and more inclined to work. For these reasons, the activities of missionaries were given limited encouragement as slavery advanced.

Some differences existed in the treatment meted out to domestic and artisan slaves on the one hand, and field slaves on the other. The former were provided with living quarters of a better quality, they were supplied with a more liberal quantity of food and clothing, and they were better treated. No greater punishment could be meted out to a domestic or artisan than to demote him or her to work in the fields.

Differences existed between rural and urban slaves, in the sense that town slaves enjoyed a greater degree of freedom than their counterparts in the country.

Field slaves were divided into gangs according to their strength and ability. The most strenuous work such as planting, digging drains, cutting canes and operating the mills was reserved for the most robust men and women, while weeding, providing fodder for the estate animals, manuring and carting were done by those who were weaker and who were incapacitated by age or ill-health. Children were employed less for the sake of their labour than to develop in them habits of hard work.

Field operations were primitive and laborious. Labour-saving devices such as ploughs and harrows were not introduced until late, if at all. Canes were planted according to the wasteful system of 'holing'. During crop time slaves worked in shifts throughout the day in order to complete milling early so as to avoid loss in the sugar content of canes. Punishment of slaves was often severe and took the form primarily of flogging since the services of the slaves were available immediately after the punishment was inflicted. This was impossible if slaves were imprisoned. In the fields, punishment was administered with a whip wielded by a driver who was himself a promoted slave and as such was often severe because of a promoted slave's tendency to give satisfactory service.

The treatment of slaves was not only cruel but also arbitrary and inconsistent. When owners were resident, the treatment tended to be better than it was when they were absent. In any case, the treatment of slaves conformed to current opinion and custom. Slaves were apt to retaliate against prolonged and very bad treatment, by arson, running away, self-inflicted maiming, suicide and rebellion. But the need to preserve society from disintegration and to prevent the loss of valuable economic resources dictated that the harsh treatment of slaves should be modified. It was realised also, that better treatment produced better work.

6. The West Indian Slave Laws with special reference to the 'Code Noir'

In the colonies of those European nations which held territory in the West Indies, and where slavery existed, a series of slave laws were adopted to regulate the lives of these slaves. In the *Spanish West Indian Colonies* the principles on which the slave laws were based, were contained in the 'Siete Partidas', a slave code which had come into existence in Spain in the 13th century, that is, long before the West Indies were discovered. The 'Siete Partidas' was not designed to deal with West Indian conditions, but they were incorporated into the laws relating to the Spanish West Indies. The *French West Indian Colonies* had another slave code applied to them. This was 'Le Code Noir' which was drawn up and passed in France. Unlike the 'Siete Partidas', the 'Code Noir' was promulgated in 1685 and dealt specifically with the problems created by slavery which had already come into existence in the French West Indies. In both the Spanish and French colonies, further laws supplemental to the codes were passed to meet changing conditions. For the *British West Indian Colonies*, there was not one single slave code. As each British colony had its own legislature, it passed its own slave laws. These laws were passed after slavery was instituted, and they were amended from time to time as conditions changed. In all three sets of laws, Spanish, British and French, despite or with amendments, the underlying principles were the same. Taken in their entirety, also, the laws based on these principles, in all three cases, tended to be more or less similar.

The nature of the slave laws passed for the Spanish, British and French colonies can be clearly seen with reference to 'Le Code Noir.' The main provisions of this Code can be divided into two categories: (*a*) the disability clauses and (*b*) the beneficent clauses.

(*a*) Disability Clauses:

   (i) Under slavery the children took the status of the mother, that is, if the mother was a slave her children were born slaves, and if the mother was free and the father was a slave her children were born free.

  (ii) Slaves were forbidden to carry arms except those who were employed by their masters in hunting.

 (iii) Slaves of different masters were not to gather together, by day or night, under pretence of weddings or otherwise.

 (iv) Slaves were forbidden on pain of the lash to sell sugar-cane even with the consent of the master. Also included in the prohibition were all kinds of provisions and firewood, etc.

  (v) A slave who struck his master, his master's wife or children in the face or causing bleeding was to be punished by death. Crimes of violence against free persons by slaves were to be severely punished, even with death.

 (vi) Thefts by slaves of horses, mules, cows, etc. might be punished with death, while thefts of less valuable things such as sheep, pigs, sugar-cane, etc. were to be punished by chastisement or branding on the shoulder.

 (vii) A slave who ran away for one month was to have his ears cut off and be branded on the shoulder for the first offence, branded on the other shoulder for the second offence, and put to death for the third offence.

(viii) Masters could claim financial compensation for slaves legally put to death. But they were also liable to make good losses caused by their slaves.

 (ix) Slaves could not legally possess property or legally make contracts.

  (x) Slaves could not fill any office or agency. They could not sue or be sued. Their evidence in court could only be used to enable the judge to understand the evidence of others, and not as proof. Slaves could be prosecuted criminally as in the case of free men.

 (xi) As personal property, slaves could be sold in debt, or bequeathed in inheritance.

(*b*) Beneficent Clauses:

  (i) All slaves in the islands were to be baptised and instructed in the Catholic religion. Sundays and holidays of the Church were to be observed.

 (ii) If a free man had children by a slave concubine he was to be fined if the slave belonged to another. He lost the slave and children if the slave belonged to him. If he married the woman, both she and the children became free.

(iii) Masters must each week supply each slave over ten years of age with two and a half pots of flour or its equivalent, two pounds of salt beef, and three pounds of fish; children under ten were to receive half the amount.

(iv) The master was to supply each slave with two linen suits or four ells of linen each year.

(v) Slaves, who were weak because of old age, sickness or otherwise, were to be cared for by their masters.

(vi) Though masters could whip their slaves or put them in irons, they were forbidden to torture or mutilate them, on pain of forfeiture and criminal prosecution.

(vii) Under the law, families were not to be broken up when slaves were sold; and slaves between forty and sixty years of age who were employed in sugar and indigo works or plantations, were deemed attached to the soil and could not be sold except with the estate.

(viii) Slaves were permitted to marry, though with their masters' consent; on the other hand, slaves could not be forced to marry if they were unwilling to do so.

(ix) Masters of twenty years of age and over could manumit (free) their slaves; but until they were twenty-five years old, they were to have the advice of relatives. Manumitted slaves were to enjoy all the rights of free subjects, though they had to respect their previous master, his widow and children.

The dictates of public security and of the personal safety of the slave owners led to the emphasis of disability over other beneficent clauses. It is worthy of note that before the beginning of the attack against the slave trade and slavery, the British West Indian slave laws had relatively few beneficent clauses. An outstanding departure from the usual type of British colonial slave laws was the law passed by the General Assembly of the Leeward Islands in 1798 entitled, 'An Act more effectively to provide for the Support and to extend certain Regulations for the Protection of Slaves, to promote and encourage their Increase, and generally to meliorate their condition.'

The disability clauses in the French slave laws, as in those of the Spanish and British, were primarily concerned with the control of runaways, the need to prevent concerted slave uprisings, the prevention and detection of thefts, the limiting of slaves' economic opportunities, and the general subordination of slaves to their masters.

Even the beneficent clauses pointed to the dependence of slaves upon their masters in the interest of public safety.

Because of the need to preserve slavery and because of the dispro-
portion between slaves and whites, the disability clauses tended to be
executed with vigour; at the same time, the beneficent clauses tended
to be neglected or laxly enforced. Manumission, for example, became
more and more difficult.

In all the West Indian colonies throughout slavery, the material
and spiritual condition of the slaves continued to be miserable.

The application of the slave laws in the Spanish, British and French
colonies at a particular time, was similar, that is, differences were those
of degree and not of kind. Generally, the treatment of slaves was
harshest in the Spanish, British, and French colonies, in the palmiest
years of sugar production in the respective colonies.

Not all of the disability clauses were enforced at all times with
equal rigour and severity. Some slave masters were humane and did
much for the moral and spiritual upliftment and for the material
welfare of their slaves. Despite laws to the contrary, for instance,
slave dances and feasts were allowed. However, the existence of the
restrictive slave laws meant that they could be enforced whenever
necessary.

As Professor Elsa Goveia concludes after her analysis of West
Indian slave laws of the 18th century, 'Both in their content and in their
enforcement, the West India slave laws follow a remarkably consistent
pattern, imposed by the function of the law in maintaining the stability
of those forms of social organisation on which rested the whole life
of the West India colonies . . .'

7. Slave Protests

Causes of Slave Protests

The protest of Negroes against their enslavement was due to one or
other of a combination of the following causes:

   (i) Desire for freedom: This was always an overriding consideration.
       Most slaves longed to be free in order to conduct their lives as
       they thought best and in their own interest.
  (ii) Harsh treatment: The unreasonable demands made upon the
       labour of slaves can be mentioned along with their excessive
       punishment, and the determination of slaves not to be reduced
       to the level of mere chattels and workhorses.
 (iii) Denial of customary rights and infringement of the minimal
       privileges of slaves, such as those relating to the supply of food,
       clothing, housing, and medical care.
  (iv) Shortage of food in time of natural disaster such as drought,
       or in time of war when imported supplies were curtailed. At

such times, slaves were inclined to protest against the difference in the amount of food available for them and for the whites.

(v) Slave dislike of a particular scheme proposed by their masters, such as for removing them from one island to another, especially if and when this involved the division of families.

(vi) Instigation of slaves by white people to protest against their masters in hope that slaves would change their allegiance.

(vii) Preponderance of slaves born in and newly arrived from Africa. Creole slaves, that is, those who were born in the West Indies into the slave system, were more likely to conform and least likely to protest.

(viii) The presence of several or many slaves of the same African tribe on the same plantation, especially if they belonged to one or other of those African tribes noted for their military prowess, for example, the Ashantis.

(ix) The emergence of a leader or leaders of quality who had the confidence of the rest of the slaves.

(x) Where, as in St. Domingue, the slaves retained their African religious practices, this served as a bond among slaves.

(xi) Outnumbering of white by slave population. For example, in Jamaica in the 17th and 18th centuries, there were approximately ten slaves to one white, and in the 19th century, there were thirteen slaves to one white; in the British Leeward Islands, generally, in the 18th century, there were eight slaves to one white. Attempts made in some British colonies to increase the white population through Deficiency Laws failed.

(xii) Landlord absenteeism and control of estates or plantations by attorneys, managers and even overseers. The treatment of slaves tended to be harsher when the owner was absent.

(xiii) Pressure in order to get rid of unpopular estate personnel. For example, in 1738, slaves on the Codrington plantation in Barbados protested against a book-keeper, who was 'a diligent Watchful Servant.' They were unsuccessful.

(xiv) The character of the white population—their inefficiency and general smugness, and their lack of vigilance. This was reflected in their neglect to provide themselves with adequate protection in terms of militias or peace-keeping corps in order to present a show of force to the slave population.

(xv) Geography: the mountainous terrain of most of the West Indian islands, with its forests, hidden passes, and ravines, was ideal as slave hideouts from which slaves could engage in guerilla warfare if attacked. The Maroons in Jamaica made full use of geographical condition in resisting capture and in establishing their independence.

(xvi) The impact of certain social or political forces. For example, the abolition movement in England, led slaves to believe that their freedom was granted by the British Government but was being withheld from them by their masters.

Forms which protests took:

  (i) Desertion, either by running away from one plantation to another where they expected better treatment, by resorting to the mountains where independent settlements were established, or by leaving the islands completely. Slaves from the British Virgin Islands and the Danish West Indies escaped to Puerto Rico where their freedom was granted.

 (ii) Suicide, either individually or in groups. Mothers invariably took their children with them. Some negroes believed that they would return to Africa after death. Some refused to eat; others ate dirt.

(iii) Malingering in the fields. Slaves were practised in the art of going slow.

(iv) Refusal to work. This was resorted to, en masse on a plantation, in groups, or individually. The return to work followed either severe flogging or concession of masters of their demands.

 (v) Feigned laziness. This was easily recognised, and so was indulged in when no one in authority was present.

(vi) Lying and insolence. These were not inherent qualities of slaves but their response to a given situation, namely, the predicament in which negroes found themselves in as slaves.

(vii) Feigning illness, or deliberately prolonging genuine illness after recovery. For example, slaves would continue to lie in hospital after they were better and until their pretences were discovered. Women tended to exploit the ailments which were peculiar to them.

(viii) Stealing, either to improve their lot, or to reduce the economic prosperity of their masters. Slaves more habitually stole from neighbouring plantations.

 (ix) The cultivation of plots and the sale of the produce in the Sunday market, and the hiring out of their labour for financial gain, were other methods used by slaves to better their condition. These were more subtle ways by which slaves resisted their lot.

 (x) Destruction of their masters' property, for example, by mutilating or ill-treating the estate animals, especially those that performed such useful functions as turning the mills, and hauling canes and sugar; by burning the fields of unripe canes, by breaking or damaging useful and expensive equipment and tools; and by burning down the house of the master if this was easy.

(xi) Self-mutilation, in order to be unable to work efficiently. For example, by cutting off of an arm or arms.
(xii) Murdering of whites by poisoning or other methods.
(xiii) Murdering other slaves in order to deprive the master of valuable property.
(xiv) Possible infanticide since infantile mortality among slaves was very high.
(xv) Rebellions or revolts. These were primarily of two kinds—spontaneous revolts which were restricted to the slaves on one estate or to those on a few neighbouring estates; planned revolts which involved or were meant to involve all of the slaves in any particular island. The objective was to overthrow the whites and assume control of the government.

8. The Revolution in St. Domingue, 1791

The revolution of St. Domingue in 1791 was an expression of protest against slavery and against the oppressive class structure which it involved. This was seen in the fact that there were two revolts, the first by the coloureds against white domination, and the second by the negro slaves who sought thereby to free themselves from the shackles of slavery.

Colour prejudice was, in part, the key to the revolution in St. Domingue. By 1789, the free coloured people in St. Domingue numbered 27,000, and they controlled a considerable part of the island's wealth. But they were denied the social and political privileges which should have accompanied such economic power. For instance, they were forbidden to hold public offices, or to engage in the learned professions. They could not acquire the patent of nobility or receive higher decorations such as the Cross of St. Louis. They were hindered from adopting European dress and habits, and they were assigned special places in theatres, inns, churches and public conveyances. As the 18th century progressed, sharper and sharper legislation had been passed against them. When a legislative Assembly was introduced in 1787, they were debarred from participating in elections either as candidates or voters. By 1791, hatred against the whites was intense.

Because of their inferiority, the slaves were oppressed to a greater extent than the free coloureds. Slaves were considered as 'things' and managed by an iron discipline. The 'Code Noir' promulgated by the French Minister Colbert in 1685, and which was revised in 1724 and 1786, was humane and set distinct bounds to the slavemaster's power. But the execution of its provisions never became a reality. The slaves enjoyed little real protection against cruel or ignorant masters. Accordingly, they sought to escape their lot by committing suicide and by running away, or to avenge themselves by damaging their masters' property, or when driven to extreme, by organising themselves in open rebellion against the whites.

Two other important considerations pertaining to the revolution of St. Domingue should be noted. By 1791, the majority of the slave population was African born; they could still remember the freedom which they had recently lost, and still desired. Also, the negroes possessed a religion and priesthood of their own, and these stimulated the desire for freedom.

Apart from the anger aroused by the social inequalities, St. Domingue was filled with discontent. Among white 'creole' Frenchmen, there was hatred of the metropolitan Frenchmen who occupied all the important offices of government. They were dissatisfied with the oppressive colonial system with its high taxation, and its denial of equal political rights to colonials. In 1788, for example, a colonial request for representatives to the proposed meeting of the States-General in France was denied. Despite this, the French 'creoles' organised themselves into a 'Colonial Committee' and proceeded to elect deputies to the States-General. France was on the brink of revolution, and because of the unstable situation there at the time, the action of the Colonial Committee was approved by the French Assembly. When this happened, agitation was started for the granting of political rights to the coloureds, and for the abolition of slavery. This agitation was led by a French society terming itself 'Amis des Noirs'. It failed, however, to achieve its objectives.

The final impetus towards revolution in St. Domingue was the outbreak of revolution in France itself in 1789. The cry of the French revolutionaries for liberty, equality and fraternity, became the aspirations of the coloureds in St. Domingue. But in 1790, the colonial whites elected themselves into a new Colonial Assembly reforming party lines among the whites only. To the coloureds this was intolerable, and the denial of their hopes became tinged with fears for their public safety.

They decided to strike for the full attainment of their political rights. The successes of the revolutionaries in France taught them the virtues of violent measures. Under the leadership of Ogé, they revolted in August, 1790. Their defeat, and the numerous executions which followed merely aroused a furious desire for revenge.

The coloured uprising and its aftermath had the double effect of throwing into further confusion an already confused situation, and by leading the negro slaves to believe that the opportunity was favourable for them to strike for freedom. On 22nd August, 1791, under the leadership of Boukman, the slaves in the vicinity of Le Cap revolted. The rising was well planned and systematically executed; the scattered white population could offer no resistance and were overwhelmed. From there the revolt spread over the North Plain and eventually engulfed St. Domingue. Under the inspired leadership of the negro Toussaint L'Ouverture, the slaves were able to establish their freedom by their defeats over the French troops sent to quell the revolt. Even when Toussaint was decoyed by the French General Le Clerc and taken as a prisoner to France, they were able to continue the struggle under Dessalines. In December, 1803, Dessalines formally proclaimed the territory's independence, renaming it Haiti, to mark its complete break with the colonial past.

The effects of the revolution of St. Domingue can be summarised as follows:

(i) The heavy losses, from yellow fever and the slaves, inflicted on the French troops assigned to suppress the revolt, depleted the forces of Napoleon and contributed to his defeat in Europe.

(ii) St. Domingue was the first territory in the Caribbean to secure political independence, but internal squabbles continued to tear the country apart and led to instability.

(iii) The economy was destroyed. For instance, the production of sugar on which the economy was based, fell from 163,405,220 lb. in 1791 to 47,600,000 lb. in 1804 to 1,896,449 lb. in 1818. Coffee production which totalled 68,151,180 lb. in 1791 fell to 20,280,589 lb. in 1818. The economy never recovered its pre-1791 viability.

(iv) From a land of large plantations, Haiti became subdivided into small peasant plots.

(v) The rigid class system of pre-revolutionary days was replaced by an equally rigid and demoralising caste system.

(vi) The revolution influenced developments elsewhere in the West Indies:

(a) The Maroon war in Jamaica in 1795 was in some way inspired by the example of St. Domingue.

(b) The surviving whites fled to the United States and to other West Indian islands such as Cuba, Jamaica and especially Puerto Rico. Jamaica owes its emergence as an important coffee producer to the French emigré coffee planters who settled there.

(c) The shortage of sugar in Europe following the outbreak of the revolution in St. Domingue, favoured the British West Indies in the immediate post-revolutionary years by increasing prices in the English and European markets. But as sugar-cane cultivation spread in Brazil, Cuba, Puerto Rico and the East Indies, and as European nations turned their attention to the production of beet sugar in response to the shortage, the British West Indian sugar industry became depressed. The economic decline of the British West Indies was partly due to the revolution of St. Domingue.

9. Arguments used for and against slavery

The adherents to slavery and the slave trade and their opponents were not without arguments to support their respective cause. These ranged from the purely emotional to the purely factual. Only the main general arguments are forwarded here; others of a secondary individual nature are omitted and no attempt has been made to justify or support any of the arguments of either party.

Against slavery

(i) On religious grounds, it was argued that slavery imposed by man was contrary to the will of God and that the subjugation and enslavement of one race by another violated the principle of the equality of man.

(ii) The capture and sale of slaves in Africa bred human jealousy and avarice and encouraged inter-tribal warfare. The passage of slaves across the Atlantic to the West Indies was fatally insanitary, slave ships were heavily congested and their cargoes subjected to disease. On the estates, the treatment of slaves was harsh and brutal. The flogging of women in particular was objectionable. The toll on human life was excessive and loss of human dignity appalling. Not only were slaves humiliated and de-humanised, but their white owners themselves were demoralised. The harshness of the system was evidenced by the many suicides, runaways and rebellions.

(iii) Slaves were improperly and badly clothed and inadequately housed and fed. The impoverished condition of slaves reduced their resistance to disease. Even so they were not offered prompt or efficient medical services.

(iv) Slavery was uneconomic and it was cheaper to operate estates by means of paid labour.

(v) The education of slaves, even religious knowledge, was neglected. The activities of missionaries who sought to Christianise slaves were discouraged and missionaries even suffered persecution by slave owners.

(vi) Justice for the slaves, especially in cases involving whites, was hardly to be expected, in a situation where judges and magistrates were themselves owners of slaves, and where slaves could not give evidence against whites.

(vii) The subordinate position of slaves, whether it was economic, social or political, was expressed in repressive colonial legislation. When it came to the rights of the slaves, however, these rights were not always similarly enshrined but were rather, in most cases, left to custom.

For slavery

(i) There was nothing immoral in slavery since, as an ancient institution, it was sanctified by time, and was also permissible by divine scripture.

(ii) The labour of slaves was essential to make plantation agriculture productive. Native Indian labour was insufficient, inadequate or lacking and white indentured labour was difficult to procure. In any case, negro labourers could best withstand the rigours of a tropical climate, while doing estate work.

(iii) Slave labour not only assisted in providing Europe with essential tropical products but helped to maintain strong national navies and mercantile marines, and to train efficient seamen employed in the trade or protection of colonies developed by slaves.

(iv) West Indian agriculture developed by slave labour, promoted British industrial development and created employment for Englishmen both at home and abroad.

(v) The treatment of slaves on West Indian plantations compared favourably with the treatment of slaves in Africa, since black African slave owners were not prompted by the same degree of enlightenment as their white European counterparts.

(vi) Slaves were provided with food, housing, clothing and medical care. Laws to regulate the distribution of these amenities were unnecessary since either simple decency or elementary economics dictated their provision. For instance, slaves represented an investment in capital which would be lost if bad feeding or inadequate medical treatment impaired their efficiency.

(vii) Considering the harshness of the time, flogging for example being a normal feature of navy life, and English children being forced to work in coal mines, the treatment of slaves was comparatively mild. It could not be excessive since the propensity of slaves to react against severe treatment by running away, by committing suicide, and by rebelling, precluded this, if the slave system was to be maintained.

(viii) Education of slaves was not necessary for them to perform estate labour but might give the slaves notions of equality which they might try to secure by violent means.

10. The struggle for the abolition of the slave trade

Slavery was abhorrent to the conscience of men from the time of its introduction in the West Indies in the 16th century. For instance, Las Casas is said to have regretted the suggestion which brought Africans across the Atlantic to replace the native Indians who were unable to satisfy the labour demands of the Spanish colonists, and whose cause he supported.

Among the first critics of slavery in the British islands were the Quakers, but these early advocates of human freedom could achieve nothing so long as West Indian agriculture provided large profits and slaves were required to work in the fields. Most people accepted the slave trade and slavery as necessary accompaniments to sugar production. Even Quakers held slaves but they were urged to treat them kindly and to free those who had given faithful service.

Towards the end of the 18th century, the institution of slavery came under increasing attack from organised groups. The final objective was the complete eradication of slavery, but the campaign envisaged definite stages. The first aim of the reformers, humanitarians, religious leaders and intellectuals, was the abolition of the slave trade. It was doubted whether in the palmy days of sugar production in the 18th century, they could have secured the emancipation of slaves; the slave trade was regarded as fair target and its abolition possible.

As is to be expected, the initiative for the abolition of the slave trade originated in England and not in the West Indies. It was too much to expect that West Indians would voluntarily bring to an end a trade which brought them profit. The first man to begin public agitation against the slave trade was Granville Sharp, an Englishman. Emboldened by his success in securing the freedom of an abandoned slave named Joseph Strong, by a court of law, Sharp decided to press for a legal decision on the question whether slavery was permitted in England. This he obtained in 1772 in the case of James Somerset a slave who had been abandoned and later reclaimed by his master. In giving his decision, the Chief Justice, Lord Mansfield said that, 'The power claimed was never in use here, nor acknowledged by the law . . . I cannot say this case is allowed or approved by the law of England'. All slaves in England thereafter became entitled to their freedom, and the way was paved for the opponents of the slave trade to organise their attack. In 1787, the Quakers formed 'The Society for Effecting the Abolition of the Slave Trade'. It was joined by such individuals as Sharp, Thomas Clarkson, and James Ramsay.

Early success was achieved. In 1788, through the efforts of Sir William Dolben who had visited a slave ship and was horrified at the conditions, a bill was passed by Parliament limiting the number of slaves to be carried in ships in proportion to their tonnage. Anti-slave trade feeling was growing but before anything further could be achieved, the French Revolution broke out in 1789, and Britain, shortly after, in 1793, found itself engaged in war with Revolutionary France. The anti-slave trade movement suffered tremendous set back from these events.

The agitation for abolition, however, was kept alive by a number of factors. The slogan ideal of 'Liberty, Equality and Fraternity' of the French revolutionists was also the objective of abolitionists. The revolt of negro slaves in St. Domingue in 1791 resulting in widespread massacre of white colonists showed what could happen in the British colonies if the slave trade and slavery were allowed to continue. In 1787, the Constitutional Convention of the United States meeting in Philadelphia, agreed that the American slave trade should end in 1807, and in 1791, the Danish Government decreed that the Danish slave trade also should cease in 1802. These were challenges to Englishmen. William Cowper's poems 'The Task' and 'The Negro's Complaint' were constant reminders to the people of the great struggle. So too was the Wedgewood Cameo, depicting a negro in an attitude of entreaty.

During the war, William Wilberforce whose part in the movement was chiefly to agitate the question in Parliament, introduced his resolution for abolition, session after session. For the first few years, however, all he was able to secure were better conditions on board slave ships. But in 1804, Wilberforce succeeded in getting the Abolition Bill passed by the House of Commons. It was defeated and thrown out by the House of Lords. In 1805, an important success was achieved when the Prime Minister, William Pitt, secured an Order in Council forbidding the importation of slaves into Trinidad and the Guiana colonies of Essequibo, Demerara and Berbice, which had recently been acquired from Spain and the Nertherlands respectively. After Pitt's death in January, 1806, his successor Charles James Fox moved a resolution for the total and immediate abolition of the slave trade. A bill to this effect was eventually passed in March, 1807, to come into force on 1st January, 1808.

The Act of Abolition provided for the end of 'all manner of dealing and trading' in slaves in Africa or their transportation to any other place. Any British subject acting illegally was to be fined £100 for every slave purchased, transported and sold, while any British ship engaging in the trade was to be seized. Rewards were offered to naval officers and others recovering slaves from such ships. Africans liberated in this way were to be under Crown protection.

The Abolition Act did not result in a complete cessation of the slave trade. The profits were too large and tempting. English traders resorted to smuggling, and further laws had to be passed. These laws were increasingly severe. In 1811, an act of Parliament made slave trading a felony and subjected those convicted to the penalty of transportation to penal settlements overseas. In 1827, slave trading was declared to be piracy and became punishable by death. The 1807 Act, however, put a legal end to slave trading. The battle for emancipation was left to be fought.

11. The aims of amelioration: its limited success

A most noticeable feature in the struggle against slavery between 1807 and 1834, was the attempt to improve the conditions under which slaves lived. The conditions of slavery were generally recognised to be bad and to bear harshly on the slaves. Failing complete emancipation, abolitionists sought to improve conditions in order to make the burden of slavery more tolerable for the slaves. Concern for the welfare of the slaves was one aspect of amelioration. Another concerned the future well-being of the slave owners themselves. Their social system seemed threatened and with it their economic survival as well. In order to counter the attacks made against them in Britain, they resorted to the amelioration plan. The policy of improving slave conditions stemmed from representatives of slave owners in London. They sought to kill adverse criticism by kindness. The idea found favour with the British Government which, after 1815, became pre-occupied with domestic social unrest and reform, and sought to promote the amelioration plan in the colonies. The final responsibility for adopting the measures rested with the colonial legislatures.

The policy of amelioration had certain clearly specified objectives which were conveyed to the colonies in a despatch from Lord Bathurst, the Secretary of State for the Colonies. The flogging of slave women was to be abolished, and there was to be one day respite before the flogging of male slaves was administered; a record of all corporal punishment exceeding three strokes was to be kept by authorised estate officials and presented quarterly to colonial magistrates. The habit of splitting slave families by sale and of selling slaves for the payment of their owners' debts was to be discontinued. The practice hitherto existing of neglecting the religious education of slaves was to be remedied by encouraging of the activities of missionaries and clergymen. Lastly, the disadvantage which slaves suffered in not being able to give evidence in courts of law was to be corrected on condition that slaves giving evidence should be sponsored by a priest or missionary.

The Secretary of State's suggestion met with a mixed reception in the British West Indian colonies according to their political system. In the Crown colonies of Trinidad, St. Lucia and Guiana (Essequibo, Demerara and Berbice), where the Crown had greater powers of intervention in introducing laws, the reforms were enforced by Orders in Council. It was otherwise in the colonies with representative assemblies. Here the reforms were successfully resisted. The fact that the proposals originated from slave owners in Britain made them no more acceptable to their counterparts who controlled the legislatures in the West Indies. Arguments against accepting the measures, though containing some measure of truth, were not unshakable. It was claimed that the colonial assemblies, like the British House of Commons, possessed sovereign rights over legislation, and that the attempt from Britain to secure the adoption of certain legislative measures, constituted a transgression of those rights. As far as the reform measures themselves were concerned, slave owners argued that these were already in opera- tion or were in the process of being introduced. On the strength of these arguments, the measures were universally rejected except for certain minor reforms.

Even in those colonies where amelioration acts were passed, there were formidable obstacles in the way of enforcement. As far as the slaves were concerned, the planters were very much the masters over them and possessed full authority on the estates. Besides, the officials who were to carry out the reforms were either slave owners themselves or were sympathetic towards the planters.

The causes for the failure or limited success of amelioration went deeper. The attitude of the British Government was important, but the need for internal reform in Britain distracted its attention from colonial affairs. Parliament was still largely controlled by landowners with sympathy for the West Indian planters, and King George IV was no abolitionist. Besides, it is probable that the British public was not fully converted or dedicated to amelioration. Amelioration was essentially a compromise and it could only appeal to those who were prepared to bargain and to compromise. West Indian slave owners did not always demonstrate their willingness to compromise.

Despite the limited success of amelioration, it was not without favourable long term benefits for the policy of emancipation generally. The failure to secure universal adoption of amelioration converted people hitherto undecided or wavering, to the cause of emancipation and swelled the ranks of emancipationists. If the slave-owners were not prepared to compromise, then the only alternative envisaged by the abolitionists was strict adherence to a policy of emancipation. Coinciding as the policy of amelioration did, with the formation of the Anti-Slavery Society in 1823, and agitation for British Parliamentary reform, its failure sealed the fate of slavery in the British West Indies.

12. Factors which aided the abolitionists and emancipationists

During the last quarter of the 18th century, the slave trade and slavery came under increasing attack in Britain. The two movements for abolition and emancipation were not inseparable: the attack on one presumed an attack on the other. Though abolition of the slave trade and the emancipation of slaves occurred at different points in time, the forces which operated to effect them were more or less similar.

Under the new evangelism introduced by John and Charles Wesley in the latter 18th century, England experienced an upsurge of religious fervour and sympathy for the welfare of mankind. In this atmosphere, the cause of the slaves could be assured of greater attention and wider public support than it had hitherto received. This change of attitude was partly the work of the missionaries, the religious sects and the humanitarians in England.

The Quakers had long agitated for an end to slavery, and in 1787 they helped to form 'The Society for Effecting the Abolition of the Slave Trade'. This Society operated through the medium of the press, popular pamphlets and the pulpit to educate the British public on the evils of slavery. Branches of the Society were formed in most large English towns. The work of the Society was supplemented by the Clapham Sect and the missionaries. The former believed that the abolition of the slave trade depended on the exercise of Christianity and the promotion of commerce and colonisation. Consequently, they assisted negroes in Britain who had drifted into idleness and destitution and established a settlement for negroes in Sierra Leone in 1787. The missionaries were a most influential group since many had served in the West Indies and had become familiar with the evils of slavery and the slave trade. Important among them were William Knibb who undertook lecture tours in England, and James Ramsay who occupied his spare time in writing pamphlets on West Indian slavery.

While the religious bodies sought to educate British public opinion, the humanitarians aimed to achieve definite gains by agitating against slavery and the slave trade in the law courts and in Parliament. In 1772, Granville Sharp, in the James Somerset case, secured the judgement of Lord Mansfield outlawing slavery in England. Thomas Clarkson secured first hand information and wrote books such as, *Is it Right to Make Men Slaves Against Their Will?* and *A Summary View of the Slave Trade and the Probable Consequences of its Abolition* which did most to denounce the evils of the slave trade. He secured many supporters including William Wilberforce who was thereafter responsible for raising the question and keeping it alive in Parliament.

In 1823, a more vigorous society was formed embracing representatives of all reforming groups. This was the 'Society for the Gradual Abolition of Slavery' or the 'Anti-Slavery Society' as it was called. It had about two hundred and twenty branches throughout England. Agitation included petitions sent to Parliament to abolish slavery, Clarkson undertook lecture tours, and in 1828 Macaulay became editor of the Society's *Anti-Slavery Monthly Reporter*, and gave vigour to its anti-slavery publications.

The success of the anti-slave trade and anti-slavery movements depended on the measure of support obtained in Parliament since parliamentary enactments were necessary to effect reform. To support his cause in Parliament, Wilberforce secured the support of Prime Ministers William Pitt and Charles James Fox, and such eminent parliamentarians as Edmund Burke. In the 1820's the formation of the Anti-Slavery Society coincided with the reforming zeal which was pervading Britain. There was a general demand for the reform of Parliament and supporters of this movement and those for emancipation gave each other mutual support. In 1830, the Tory Government was replaced by a Whig Government which was more amenable to reform. They were supported by King William IV who succeeded George IV that year, and together they passed the Emancipation Act in August, 1833.

Economic conditions also favoured the abolitionists and emancipationists. The principal cities engaged in the slave trade, namely, London, Bristol and Liverpool, had developed other economic interests than slave trading and did not fear the loss from abolition. For example, Liverpool had a new interest in the importation of raw cotton from the United States of America for the mills of Lancashire which could compensate for the loss of the slaves. The early 19th century was a period of depression in West Indian agriculture. Declining profitability served to weaken the opposition from the West India Interest in Britain, who agitated against abolition and emancipation, in and out of Parliament.

The declining influence of West Indian planters has also to be seen within the context of conflicting economic interests in Britain. Traditionally, the great landowners were the ruling class but by the 19th century, a new group of influential men had emerged. These were the industrialists and manufacturers, the product of the Industrial Revolution. These men had little sympathy with the slave trade and slavery especially since they were attracted by the more lucrative market for their textile and metal products in the East Indies. Slavery was doomed when these men came to dominate Parliament in 1832. The conflict of interest between the agricultural and industrial classes further represented a clash between two ideologies, that of traditional monopoly and that of emergent *laissez faire* and freedom of trade. The victory of the latter over the former signified the victory of industrialists over agriculturalists and spelt doom for the slave trade and slavery.

13. Provisions of the Act of Emancipation

The 'Act for the Abolition of Slavery throughout the British Colonies; for promoting the Industry of the Manumitted Slaves; and for compensating the persons hitherto entitled to the Services of such Slaves' was passed by the British Parliament in August, 1833 and brought into effect on 1st August, 1834. Its provisions constituted a guide to colonial legislatures to pass ancillary acts on similar terms.

(i) From 1st August, 1834, slavery was to be 'utterly and forever abolished and declared unlawful throughout the British Colonies.'

(ii) Slave children under six years of age, and all children born to slave mothers were to be free. Exceptions were children between twelve and twenty-one who were destitute—these might be apprenticed out.

(iii) All other slaves were to serve a period of apprenticeship to their masters: in the case of praedials (field slaves) until 1st August, 1840, and non-praedials (non-field slaves) until 1st August, 1838.

(iv) Apprentices were to work for three-quarters of the working week for their masters; for the remainder of the week they could labour for their own benefit, or if they preferred, for their master but for agreed wages.

(v) The apprenticeship might be brought to an end before the specified time either by voluntary discharge by the master, or by purchase by the apprentice. Freedom could be purchased even against the wishes of the master. In case of voluntary discharge, the master was to remain responsible for the care of aged and infirm apprentices during the remaining portion of their apprenticeship.

(vi) The apprentice was to continue to be provided by his master with 'food, clothing, lodging, medicine, medical attendance, and such other Maintenance and Allowance' as he was accustomed to have during slavery. If food was not supplied, then the apprentice should be provided with adequate provision grounds and leisure time to grow his own food.

(vii) The apprentice was bound to work honestly, to refrain from insolence and insubordination, and to abandon all attempts to escape the fulfilment of his contract.

(viii) The 'effectual Superintendence' of the apprentices and jurisdiction over them was entrusted to Stipendiary Magistrates who were to be paid £300 a year from the British Treasury.

(ix) Slave-owners were to be compensated for the loss of their property in slaves, and a grant of £20 million was allocated by the British Government for this purpose.

14. Emancipation in the French West Indies

Shortly after the outbreak of the French Revolution, slavery was abolished within the French West Indies. But it was reimposed by Napoleon when he came into power, and retained by the Bourbon kings of France when they were restored in 1815. Only in St. Domingue (or Haiti) because of the revolution, was there no slavery.

The general progression towards emancipation in the French West Indies was almost similar to that in the British West Indies.

The French slave trade was abolished in 1818.

Following a number of slave rebellions in Martinique in 1822, 1824 and 1833, the French Government adopted a policy of amelioration. The non-existence until 1834 of legislative assemblies in the French colonies which could thwart the intention of the mother country, enabled the French Government to carry through its policy. But in 1832, the tax on manumission was abolished while the procedures for achieving manumission were simplified. Henceforth it became easier for slaves to buy their freedom. In 1833, measures were adopted for the compulsory registration of slaves, and some of the grosser forms of punishment such as mutilation and branding were prohibited. In 1836 slavery was outlawed in France. Slaves carried there from the West Indies became free on arrival.

Amelioration, however, was only a stop-gap policy. In any case, the opposition from French West Indian planters and sympathetic officials negated benefits anticipated from the measures passed. It became evident that full emancipation was the only answer to slavery.

In 1834, the French 'Societe pour l'abolition de l'esclavage' was formed, and by 1838 it was sufficiently strong to introduce in the French Assembly the first legislation to end slavery. However, the measure was successfully resisted by representatives of the French West India Interest in the Assembly.

The spirit of reform in France in the 1840's, stirred by socialist zeal, greatly facilitated the movement for emancipation. In 1848, the year of revolution in France, the Act for emancipation was passed. Slaves in the French colonies became free unconditionally,—there was no period of apprenticeship. That was unique to the British West Indies.

Conclusion

The Spaniards first tried the native Indians as labourers, but when these proved inadequate, turned to negro labour. Other Europeans at first tried European indentured labourers, but when these could not be obtained in sufficient numbers, they had recourse to negro Africans also. Negroes were employed as slaves.

Slavery had a profound effect upon West Indian society. It led to the emergence of various social groups—the whites, the free negroes and free coloureds, and slaves—based on qualities of colour, wealth and education. Within each group there were further subdivisions. The free negroes and free coloureds and slaves occupied inferior social positions, and they were denied equal political and economic privileges to the whites.

The living and working conditions of slaves in particular were bad. Food and clothing were inadequate, and housing was far below the standards of those belonging to the whites. Education was neglected. Punishment for offences, however minor, was harsh and brutal. Generally, the treatment meted out to domestic and artisan slaves was better than that meted out to field slaves. Also, urban slaves had more privileges than rural slaves.

Slavery attracted the attention of humane Europeans at an early date, but it was not until the late 18th century that conditions favoured their efforts to abolish the slave trade and slavery. In England, a new evangelism and the formation of religious societies, the Industrial Revolution and the emergence of a new industrial and manufacturing class, together with the reforming zeal of the British Government and the growth of the concept of *laissez faire*, all militated against slavery and aided the abolitionists. Against these forces, the resistance of the West India Interest was weak and of no avail because of their declining economic condition. In 1808 the British slave trade was abolished, and after a futile attempt by the British Government to get British West Indians to accept laws for the amelioration of harsh slave conditions, the Act of Emancipation was passed in 1833. This freed all slaves under six years of age and introduced a period of apprenticeship for the others.

In its progression from the abolition of the slave trade through amelioration to the emancipation of slaves, the movement to deal with slavery in the French colonies resembled the movement to deal with slavery in the British colonies. The fundamental difference was that while the slaves in the French colonies did not have to undergo a period of apprenticeship, their counterparts in the British colonies had to do so.

Revision Questions

1. Why were negro slaves introduced in the West Indies?
2. How were slaves obtained in Africa, and what hardships did they undergo on the way to the West Indies?
3. What arguments were used to justify slavery? What counter arguments could be made?
4. Why and how was the British slave trade abolished in 1808?
5. Describe the main social groups which made up a typical West Indian colony in the 18th century.
6. By 1833 slavery in the British colonies was doomed. Explain this statement.

4. The Apprenticeship System

The term 'emancipation' which was used to describe the Act of 1833 passed by the British Government to put an end to slavery in the British Empire, is ambiguous and misleading. Slaves were not freed in the sense that they were given unrestricted control over their freedom of movement. Rather, they had to serve a period of apprenticeship unless the local legislatures decided to dispense with it. And apprenticeship was neither one thing nor another: it was neither full freedom nor was it full slavery. Apprentices were bound to the estates by regulations which laid down compulsory residence and work as in the days of slavery. Only for a part of the week could apprentices work for themselves. If they preferred to use their free time to work for their masters, they would do so for wages. The conditions of slavery and of freedom which apprenticeship possessed nullified many of the advantages which were expected of the system. For example, compulsory labour gave too little experience in working for wages. Generally, the position of the apprentices was too weak to enable them to bargain with their masters about conditions of employment. The position of the planters, however, remained strong. Accordingly, they sought to extract as much labour out of the apprentices before, in their opinion, the final ruin of full freedom set in.

The disadvantages of apprenticeship would have been more marked but for the activities of the Stipendiary Magistrates. These men were appointed to execute certain provisions of the Act of Emancipation and the colonial enactments which gave effect to it. But not even these men who administered, more or less, an impartial justice, were able to correct the shortcomings of an inadequate system.

Apprenticeship failed to satisfy. This became apparent to all concerned, namely, the apprentices and their masters in the West Indies, and the British Government and humanitarian groups in Britain. Hence all were in favour of an early end to the system. In 1838, two years before the scheduled time, apprenticeship for all apprentices was brought to an end in all the British colonies. Partial slavery gave way to full freedom.

1. The aims of apprenticeship and how far they were realised

Wherever it was introduced in the British West Indies, apprenticeship had three main aims: it was intended to provide an easy and peaceful transition from slavery to freedom; it sought to guarantee the planters an adequate supply of labour during the period it lasted; and it was expected to train the apprentices for the responsibilities of freedom, especially in working regularly for wages. The extent to which these aims were realised varied from island to island and sometimes in different parts of the same island, according to the peculiarities of geography and soil, and to the outlook of the planters concerned.

In none of the colonies was apprenticeship marked by violent disturbance of the public order. Planters showed good sense by allowing themselves to be guided by the directions of the British Government; their receipt of the compensation money depended upon this. The paternal attitude of the British Government tended to alleviate the grievances of some apprentices, for example, as these related to hours of work and the length of the working day. Acute friction between planters who sought to extract the maximum labour from apprentices, and the apprentices who sought to escape plantation labour under the impression that they had been freed in 1834, was avoided by the adjudication of differences by the Stipendiary Magistrates.

According to the laws governing apprenticeship, the apprentices were forced to work for their masters for three quarters of the working week. There is no evidence that the estates suffered from a lack of labour. It is true that in ten out of eleven British West Indian colonies there was a decline in sugar production during apprenticeship. But this should not be attributed to shortage of labour. The 1830's witnessed a continuation of a depression in the sugar industry which had existed since the beginning of the 19th century. Apprenticeship was not a factor contributing to the depression. Rather, but for apprenticeship and the forced labour it provided, the decline in sugar production would have been more marked. Apprenticeship tended to sustain production and made the decline less acute than it would have normally been.

As a means of giving the apprentices relevant training for freedom, apprenticeship was weakened by the large element of coercion which was left in it. Apprenticeship was nothing but a modified slavery and apprentices did not have full power to bargain with the planters the conditions of labour. From this failing developed one of the worst disadvantages of the period, namely, the emergence of new elements of friction between future employers and employees. After the apprenticeship period ended, labour relations were to be marked by continued mutual suspicions and distrust.

The social development of the apprentices suffered similar neglect to the economic. The British Government was willing to give freedom to the slaves, but it was not prepared to spend the sum necessary for the establishment of a new society. Nor did it enforce this responsibility on the slave-owners. Here was evidenced the working of the principle of *laissez faire*, namely, that each person should be given the opportunity to work out his own destiny unfettered by restrictions or interference, and alternatively, that such persons should require no assistance. As a Governor of Trinidad put it in 1848, '. . . a race has been freed but a society has not been formed'. In 1833, the British Government gave a grant of £30,000 for the education of negroes. But the scheme failed from an acute shortage of teachers and from the lack of any idea of how to utilise the fund beneficially.

2. The role of the Stipendiary Magistrates and the difficulties they encountered

As a result of imperial legislation, the system of slavery in the British West Indies was abandoned in August, 1834, for a system of apprenticeship to last for a definite period. One innovation of the Emancipation Act of 1833 was the appointment of Stipendiary Magistrates.

According to Lord Stanley, the Secretary of State for the Colonies, the Stipendiary Magistrates should be 'men uninfluenced by the local assemblies, free from local passions'. Accordingly, most of them were appointed from Britain, and since one of the intentions of the British Government was to keep down costs, the great majority were appointed from among retired army and naval officers living on half-pay. It was assumed that these men were particularly qualified because they were accustomed to rough conditions in various parts of the world, and because they were accustomed to enforcing discipline. In addition to these men, a smaller number of non-officials from Britain, as well as some white and coloured West Indians not associated with the planter or merchant class, were appointed. This system of appointing Stipendiary Magistrates was adopted to prevent the administration of apprenticeship from falling into the hands of the slave-owners.

Stipendiary Magistrates were expected to administer justice and to assist in preventing social and economic disturbance. The lack of justice towards slaves in the British West Indies made it essential that the provisions governing apprenticeship should be administered by men who were untainted by the plantation system and who were expected to perform impartially. They were to ensure that both owners and apprentices secured their respective rights under the law.

The Stipendiary Magistrates had a second equally important function. Prior to the introduction of the apprenticeship system, the fear of civil disorder leading to the outbreak of violence against the white colonists, and of the collapse of plantation agriculture, was widespread in the British West Indian colonies and to a lesser extent in England. The appointment of Stipendiary Magistrates was made in order that they might help to preserve public peace and order, and to alleviate this fear.

The two functions of Stipendiary Magistrates were inter-related and this was expressed in the nature of the duties they had to perform.

The Stipendiary Magistrates' main duty was to supervise the operation of the Act of Emancipation and such colonial enactments which gave effect to it. They were given the exclusive jurisdiction over offences committed by the apprentices or by their employers in relation to each other. In some colonies, the Stipendiary Magistrates' jurisdiction extended even to minor offences, such as petty thefts, which were not within the relations between master and apprentice. For the purpose of settling differences, they had to visit the various estates in their district at regular intervals. They dealt with a multitude of cases ranging from charges made against the apprentices of insolence, laziness and insubordination, to counter-charges against the owners of severity, assault, inadequate medical treatment and cheating in the matter of working hours. Before they left the estates, the Stipendiary Magistrates had to ensure that no one was imprisoned without their orders and that medical attention was given to apprentices in hospitals. In some colonies, Stipendiary Magistrates had to inspect jails and work-houses, and in all colonies they had to assist in fixing the value of negroes who wanted to buy their freedom. The duties of the Stipendiary Magistrates were not confined only to those enacted but, in addition, included instructions given to them from time to time by the Governors or their representatives.

The wide range of their duties naturally imposed a severe strain on the Stipendiary Magistrates, many of whom were incapacitated by old age and sickness. The regular visiting of estates was the most arduous and most unpleasant part of their work especially as climatic conditions were unfamiliar and hostile to them. Their duties entailed a great deal of travelling and that, especially in the mountains with improper roads, could be painful and even fatal. No provision for housing was made for Stipendiary Magistrates on overnight duty to remote estates.

Conditions of employment were discouraging. For the first year, the salary of Stipendiary Magistrates was £300 sterling each but their expenses far exceeded this amount. Their financial position improved from July 1835, when they received a travel and housing allowance of £150 sterling annually. Even so they had to exercise the strictest economy to make ends meet. If Stipendiary Magistrates died in service, there was no pension for their dependents. If they were invalided out of service, or were dismissed, they had to pay their own passage home. There was no sick leave. These examples of bad working conditions explain why some Stipendiary Magistrates performed their work unsatisfactorily and why some fell prey to the inducements offered by the planters.

No Stipendiary Magistrate who performed his duties conscientiously could have much leisure for body or mind. Stipendiary Magistrates had been given specific and important tasks to perform but they were not put in a position of being able to carry them out fully. One result of their rigorous conditions of service was that many Stipendiary Magistrates died in office and nearly all suffered severe illness. Some preferred just to resign.

If Stipendiary Magistrates acquired a reputation as friends of apprentices, such as Norcott and Hill of Jamaica, or when it was evident that they were not amenable to the wishes of the employers, hostility towards them, already latent, developed rapidly. They were persecuted and obstructed in the performance of their duties. The minute attention directed to their activities by such bodies as the missionaries, the Anti-Slavery Society, the West India Committee, the Colonial Office, Parliament, and planters and their associates, and the criticisms sometimes offered from all quarters made it difficult for them to perform their duties properly.

3. An assessment of the work of the Stipendiary Magistrates

The limited success which apprenticeship achieved was due to a large extent to the work of the Stipendiary Magistrates. As a result of their achievements and despite their failings, they came to be called the 'architects of freedom'.

The activities of the Stipendiary Magistrates accounted in large measure for the peaceful transition of apprenticeship, thereby reducing the fears of those who had predicted violence and destruction. Stipendiary Magistrates could be approached by both apprentices and their masters, and presented with their complaints. In their adjudication of differences, and in merely listening to petitions, they acted as a safety-valve for the tensions of society. Had these tensions been allowed to accumulate they could have destroyed the system.

Regular contact with the Stipendiary Magistrates served to inform the apprentices of their rights and duties as no other medium could. For instance, the apprentices did not have to depend on gossip or an occasional newspaper to learn of their rights. In this way, the Stipendiary Magistrates could allay suspicions and misunderstandings, which might otherwise have led to violence and rebellion.

The success of the Stipendiary Magistrates can be measured by the many acts of oppression which they prevented or mitigated. They acted as the buffer between two groups with conflicting interests and kept them together. One source of continuous friction was wages. Many masters wanted to pay what wages they cared to give and when they liked. Apprentices objected, and the matter had to be settled by the Stipendiary Magistrates. Similarly they had to deal with disputes over hours of work. Planters tended to count working hours from when the apprentices arrived in the fields. Apprentices wanted the time taken to reach the work place to be counted also.

The administration of the laws by the Stipendiary Magistrates removed the apprentices from the prejudice and tyranny of the planter-dominated magistrates and Justices of the Peace who during slavery had executed an arbitrary justice. But, the persecution of Madden by the Council of Kingston in Jamaica showed what could happen to a Stipendiary Magistrate who wanted to exercise justice.

In many cases, the advice of the Stipendiary Magistrates enabled the apprentices to organise their lives better, and so, in some measure, prepared them for the challenges of full freedom. The work of William Gordon in the Virgin Islands should be noted in this respect. His advice to apprentices, freely and continuously given, greatly clarified their approach to the new life after apprenticeship.

Undoubtedly, some Stipendiary Magistrates performed unsatisfactorily, but the general success of the system proves that a reasonable number of them must have been guided by the highest ideals of their office. When failure occurred, it could be ascribed in most cases to circumstances beyond their control.

But the heavy demands made on the Stipendiary Magistrates undoubtedly impaired their efficiency, and the rigours of their employment must have strained their allegiance to the utmost. Some of them fell under the influence of the local plantocracy and where this happened the interests of the apprentices necessarily suffered.

The Stipendiary Magistrates were so over-burdened with the need to attend to petty differences between apprentices and employers that they had little time to formulate and implement schemes for the improvement of the social conditions of the apprentices. In spite of their attention to duty, they could not prevent the corporal punishment of apprentices.

The Stipendiary Magistrates never succeeded in dominating the social life of the colonies. This is understandable. They were too few—a total of 132 being finally appointed to all the colonies; the resident whites were too firmly established; and their operations were limited by the Imperial Act of Emancipation and by the supporting ancillary acts of the colonies.

The effectiveness of the Stipendiary Magistrates was further impaired by their weak economic position which made it impossible for them to live on equal terms with the resident whites. They could not return hospitality offered to them and so could not accept it without prejudice to their position of impartiality.

Summing up the work of the Stipendiary Magistrates in the British West Indies, W. L. Burn states, 'On the tone of West Indian life as a whole they had too little effect, for the conditions of their service placed them on the defensive and made them glad if they held their own, avoid unnecessary trouble and keep their health'.

4. The end of apprenticeship

According to the Emancipation Act of 1833, domestic slaves were to serve an apprenticeship of four years, and field slaves were to serve for six years. This meant that for domestic and field apprentices, apprenticeship would last until 1st August, 1838 and 1st August, 1840, respectively. As envisaged by the architects of the Act, therefore, full freedom for all the apprentices would not come until 1840. Nevertheless, when in 1838 domestic apprentices obtained their freedom, a similar privilege was extended to the field apprentices. Several factors were responsible for the ending of the apprenticeship of field workers two years before the specified time.

(i) Some planters envisaged definite gains. It would no longer be necessary to provide the apprentices with food, clothes, medical care and housing. At the same time they would pay the lowest wages which would be necessary to attract just the number of labourers required in and out of crop. Henceforth, also, the wage-earner would be responsible for the physical and spiritual welfare of himself and his family.

(ii) The British Government was beginning to have doubts about the benefits of apprenticeship and that the scheme was not providing the apprentices with the kind of training for freedom which was envisaged. Its doubts were confirmed by the findings in Jamaica of a Royal Commission appointed to investigate the operation of apprenticeship in the British West Indies.

(iii) As the end of apprenticeship for domestic workers approached, the Anti-Slavery Society began to agitate as in pre-emancipation days by holding public meetings and circulating pamphlets showing the faults and exposing the evils of apprenticeship.

(iv) The humanitarians were convinced that the apprentices had not yet experienced the benefits of freedom and by 1838 were arguing that it was time that they should do so.

(v) By 1838, also, all apprentices—field-workers as well as domestics—were looking forward to being free. In some cases, they were taught by the Stipendiary Magistrates to expect this. To withhold freedom from the field-apprentices could have led to much dissatisfaction and possibly violence.

(vi) In some colonies, it was difficult to differentiate between the domestic and field apprentices. As a result of the shortage of field labourers, it was necessary to supplement the labour force by recruitment from among the domestics. If, therefore, the domestics working in the fields obtained their freedom, the regular field slaves would also claim their freedom. The system was, accordingly, fraught with danger and threatened to collapse from opposition by the field slaves. In order to avert this danger, it was decided that apprenticeship for both domestic and field-workers should end at the same time on 1st August, 1838.

5. Problems facing the West Indies after 1838

British West Indian agriculture was in decline even before emancipation and continued after it. This was due primarily to the wasteful and inefficient methods of production, an inadequate market, soil exhaustion, excessive competition for the limited market, bad management, low prices and shortage of capital.

Emancipation disrupted the traditional labour system and was followed by a number of problems which led to further depression and which called for attention, if the production of the staple products was to be continued.

Emancipation converted people who were hitherto slaves and apprentices into free people whose labour could be obtained only by paying them agreed wages. But currency was in small supply. That part of the £20 million obtained by British West Indian planters from the slaves compensation fund was expended in paying off debts and in buying capital equipment such as ploughs to do the work previously done by slaves. West Indian banks were not firmly established and collapsed soon after emancipation. Also, following the financial and commercial crises in Britain around 1847, the British banks which had hitherto provided capital to West Indian planters, traders and merchants, failed in turn. Moreover, Englishmen with capital were not willing to invest in the West Indies but preferred the East Indies whose soils were more fertile and whose productive capacity was greater.

The shortage of capital was aggravated by the low prices obtained for sugar, which between 1838 and 1847 fell from 33/8 per cwt. to 23/8 per cwt. in London. Prices fell even further after 1847, and by 1854 were only 21/5 per cwt.

Production was affected by a succession of natural disasters, the hurricane of 1837 being followed by further hurricanes and droughts in the 1840's. The destruction of crops deprived the planters of needed capital; this money was doubly necessary, not only for the ordinary running of the estates, but also to restore damaged works and buildings.

The shortage of capital meant that employers could only pay low wages and this in turn affected the labourers' willingness to work on the plantations. In the small islands where plantation agriculture dominated the economy and where there was little land for further cultivation, the ex-slaves were compelled to work on the estates, but in large territories like Guiana, Trinidad and Jamaica where there was plenty of idle land, the ex-slaves established themselves on plots away from estates and were content to work for only limited periods for the subsistence wages then offered. For the most part, they preferred to work on their own plots. Women preferred to attend to their homes and children.

In an attempt to meet this uncertain labour supply, planters adopted the 'metairie' system by which they sought to attract labourers by offering them a share of the profits. By metairie, also, planters could pay wages in kind rather than in cash while the labourers shared with them the risks and expenses of production. But metairie failed because the labourers did not receive their fair share of the proceeds of their labour. Thus the drift away from the estates continued.

To meet the shortage of labour, the planters resorted to the immigration of indentured labourers. Africans were tried but they soon followed the ex-slaves in leaving the plantations. Chinese and Portuguese were also brought but they proved bad labourers and set themselves up in business after their term of indenture ended. Only the Indian indentures proved successful but an initial reluctance of the British Government to encourage their immigration had to be overcome. The efforts of the Indians revived the failing fortunes in the sugar industry especially in Guiana and Trinidad, and to a lesser extent in Jamaica, where they were imported in large numbers. In Guiana, for instance, where sugar production had fallen from 60,000 tons in 1830 to 23,000 tons in 1846, there was an increase to 92,000 tons by 1871.

After emancipation, as before, West Indian sugar met with increasing competition from East Indian (for example, Mauritian and Indian) sugar in the British market, and from European beet sugar which competed with the continental and British markets. The effect of competition from East Indian sugar was reflected in the Sugar Duties Act of 1846 which in stages made the duties on all sugar entering Britain the same. Preferences given to West Indian planters were thereby removed. More serious was the competition from beet sugar, producers of which received a special incentive from their governments in the form of bounties. It was not until 1903 that West Indian planters obtained a partial relief from beet sugar competition when the British Government prohibited the importation of bounty-fed beet sugar into Britain.

The problems of West Indian agriculture after 1838 were largely due to an excessive reliance upon a one-crop economy. Very little attempt was made to diversify agriculture and it was not until after 1898 when a West Indian Department of Agriculture was established, following the recommendations of a Royal Commission, that attempts were made to introduce a diversified economy.

Conclusion

In the British West Indies, the Act of Emancipation which came into effect on 1st August, 1834, did not introduce full freedom. It introduced a period of apprenticeship, or partial freedom, instead. Field slaves were to serve an apprenticeship until 1840 and the others an apprenticeship until 1838.

Apprenticeship was successful in providing the estates with adequate labourers and there was no major eruption of violence while it lasted, but it did not help to prepare apprentices for the responsibilities of full freedom, nor did it improve their social conditions.

An important innovation of the Emancipation Act was the introduction of Stipendiary Magistrates who were to be unconnected with the slave system. They were expected to supervise the operation of the Emancipation Act and adjudicate in differences between masters and apprentices. But the terms of their employment, for example, their inadequate salaries, their many duties, their inadequate housing and travel allowances, and their relationship with the white colonists, made their work difficult. However, it is undoubted that their endeavours resulted in the smooth transition from slavery to freedom.

Apprenticeship was an unsatisfactory system. Planters saw definite economic advantages to be had from full freedom, humanitarian groups believed that apprentices should experience the social benefits of freedom, while all apprentices, domestic as well as field workers, were looking forward to be fully free in 1838. Accordingly, all apprenticeship was brought to an end in August, 1838, two years before the majority of apprentices who were field-workers, were scheduled to receive full freedom.

With the introduction of full freedom in 1838, one phase of British West Indian history was brought to an end. At about the same time that slavery was receiving the attention of the British Government, active consideration was being given to another aspect of West Indian society, namely, the system of government.

Revision Questions

1. What were the chief features of apprenticeship?
2. Why was apprenticeship not completely successful?
3. From the chapter and from your own reading, describe what provisions were made for the education of negroes during this period, and what success was achieved?
4. Why were Stipendiary Magistrates called 'the architects of freedom'?
5. Were the difficulties experienced by Stipendiary Magistrates of their own making?
6. What arguments can be made for and against 'full freedom' on 1st August, 1838?

5. Colonial Government

While the West Indian islands after their settlement were of doubtful or unknown benefit to interested European governments, or while they required capital for their development which these governments could ill-afford, they were allowed to remain under the control and direction of private individuals. After his discovery of the West Indies, Christopher Columbus was created 'Admiral and Viceroy and Governor therein' but his direct responsibilities to the Spanish Crown were not detailed. In the English and French colonies, the Crown transferred its responsibilities to Lords-Proprietors and to 'directeurs' respectively. The Crown wielded minimum control, leaving it to those authorised to frame regulations for the management of colonial matters.

The state of transferred responsibility remained for a shorter period in the Spanish than in the non-Hispanic colonies. However, the ensuing changes in systems of government were influenced by the same general condition in all of them, namely, the potentials of wealth, known or assumed, which the colonies possessed, either in the form of precious metals or of tropical agricultural products. In the English and French colonies, the change came largely as a consequence of the introduction of large-scale sugar production for export.

In the British West Indies, the authority of the Lords-Proprietors was replaced by that of the Privy Council (representing the British Government) operating through a department of government. At first, from 1660, colonial matters were handled by the Council for Foreign Plantations and the Council of Trade. In 1672, these two Councils were combined to form the Council of Trade and Plantations which, in turn, was eventually to evolve into the Colonial Office under the Secretary of State for the Colonies, in the later 18th century.

With the change in the system of colonial government from Lord-Proprietor to British Government, the colonial governors hitherto appointed by the Lord-Proprietor were appointed by the Crown and became royal representatives in their respective colonies. They continued to be assisted by councils and assemblies.

The colonial political system was a replica of the system existing in the mother-country. And an essential feature of colonial legislatures was their assumption of rights and privileges equal to those of their European counterparts. Colonial legislatures did not willingly accept a subordinate position to the imperial parliaments. Any suspicion by the colonial legislatures of interference with their political rights by the imperial government aroused resistance and retaliation. In the British colonies, the unwillingness of the planter-legislators to accept and implement suggestions of social improvement for slaves and ex-slaves, and their general recalcitrance resulted in the change from representative to Crown Colony Government whereby the Crown could exercise a greater controlling influence over colonial affairs.

1. The Government of the Spanish American Empire

Four general aims governed the policy of the Spanish Crown in its American Empire: to spread the Catholic religion, to draw the maximum possible revenue compatible with good administration, to assert and extend its direct authority, and to administer justice. By the middle of the 16th century, not only had these main lines of Crown policy been clearly indicated, but the main instruments for enforcement had been chosen. Success depended upon replacing the self-appointed captains and governors of the initial conquest by reliable officials appointed by the Crown.

The Spanish-American Empire was governed by and through several agents or agencies in Spain and in the colonies themselves. In Spain there were the Royal and Supreme Council of the Indies, and the House of Trade (Casa de Contratacion). In the colonies, there were the Viceroys or Captains-General, the audiencias, the provincial governors, and the cabildos.

The Council of the Indies, the supreme body, was previously a standing committee of the Council of Castile, but it was given a separate existence in 1524. It was composed of lawyers and clergy learned in civil law. The Council had complete control over matters in Spanish America relating to laws, courts, trade, commerce, finance, defence, and appointment of the higher clergy. It appointed and supervised the conduct of all royal officials from Viceroys downwards who were sent to the colonies. The Council also acted as the final court of appeal from decisions of the colonial audiencias. Under its direction, and especially during the 17th century, elaborate codes of law covering every branch of government were issued for the colonies. Finally, the Council exercised powers of censorship, that is, no book on the colonies could be printed in Spain or in the colonies themselves without its inspection, approval and license, and no book might be introduced into the colonies without its express permission.

The House of Trade was exclusively responsible for the adoption and enforcement of measures for the regulation and development of trade and commerce. Its duty was to ensure that Spanish colonial trade remained the preserve of Spaniards and that it was conducted in the interest of Spain. It was responsible for licensing all ships and merchants, and supervising passengers, cargoes, crews and equipment passing between Spain and the colonies. It received the customs duties, the convoy tax and other trade revenues collected.

The Viceroy or Captain-General exercised supreme authority within his colonial jurisdiction as the direct representative of the Spanish sovereign. He was the chief civil and military officer. He supervised the administration of justice, the exchequer and certain aspects of the work of the church. He was specifically charged with the maintenance and increase of royal revenue. In addition, he nominated most of the minor colonial officials, both lay and ecclesiastic. The welfare of the Indians was presumed to be his special care—he was expected to consider Indian petitions, listen to suits involving Indians and re-allot vacant ecomiendas.

Each Vice-royalty was subdivided into audiencias. Each audiencia was administered by a council of lawyers appointed from Spain. They acted both in a judicial and an administrative capacity. Judicially, they dealt with both civil and criminal law suits. They acted as supreme courts and heard and decided appeals from inferior tribunals. In criminal cases the decision of the audiencia was final, that is, there was no re-appeal to Spain. But important civil suits might be re-appealed to the Council of the Indies. Administratively, the audiencias protected the interests of the aborigines by listening to suits involving Indians. Also, they advised the Viceroy on matters of general policy and administration and at the same time watched to see that he committed no illegalities or oppression.

For purposes of local administration, the audiencias were divided into provinces. Governors were put in charge and they held office for three to five years. The governor was the political leader of the province, its legislator in matters of local policy, generally the commander-in-chief of its military establishment if there was one, and its most important judicial officer. In the course of his term of office, the governor had to make one tour of his province, informing himself about local administration of justice and government, hearing cases and taking

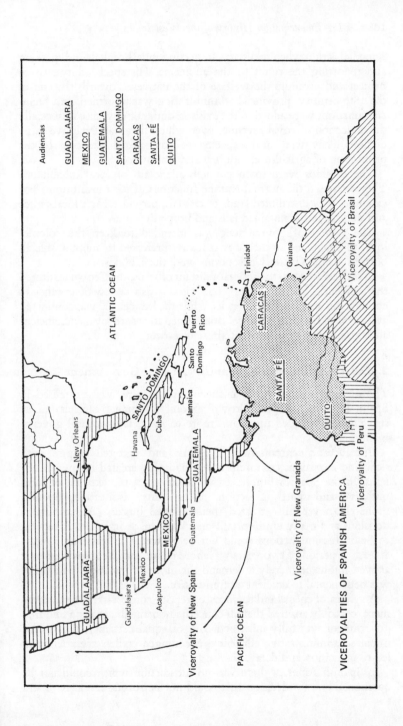

Audiencias

GUADALAJARA

MEXICO

GUATEMALA

SANTO DOMINGO

CARACAS

SANTA FÉ

QUITO

ATLANTIC OCEAN

Trinidad

Guiana

Puerto Rico

Santo Domingo

Jamaica

Cuba

Havana

SANTO DOMINGO

New Orleans

GUADALAJARA

Guadalajara

Mexico

Acapulco

MEXICO

Guatemala

GUATEMALA

CARACAS

SANTA FÉ

QUITO

Viceroyalty of New Granada

Viceroyalty of Peru

Viceroyalty of Brasil

Viceroyalty of New Spain

PACIFIC OCEAN

VICEROYALTIES OF SPANISH AMERICA

remedial action when necessary, inspecting inns, hospitals and markets, and reporting the result to the audiencia. His special duty was to protect and promote the welfare of the natives. Towards the end of the 18th century, provincial administration was reformed, and financial functions were added to the existing duties of governors, especially the collection of royal revenue, over which they had exclusive jurisdiction. They were also expected to pay special attention to the promotion of agriculture, industry and commerce.

The cabildos were town councils made up of local inhabitants. They exercised the normal routine functions of such institutions. For example, they distributed lands to citizens, provided for a local police and militia, and maintained jails and hospitals.

The system of government was intended to keep the colonies loyal to Spain, and so the Crown always preferred to appoint officials born in Spain. The only exceptions were the cabildos.

In order to control the action of distant officials, the Crown instituted the 'residencia' and the 'visita'. The 'visita' was a review of an official's conduct during his term of service while the 'residencia' was conducted at the end of his term of office. Both aimed to ensure loyal and efficient administration and to prevent abuse of power.

2. Defects and merits of Spanish Colonial Government

The government of the Spanish colonial empire was centralised in Spain. Not only did the Crown appoint the higher officials but its surveillance extended more and more to the details of local government.

Bureaucratic centralisation in a vast and scattered empire with slow and hazardous communications naturally created its own problems. In the Spanish Empire it was achieved at the expense of local initiative and speed of action. With some justification, Spanish monarchs never fully trusted their colonial officers. All important decisions and many unimportant ones were made in Spain. A request to Spain for instructions could not be answered in less than a year, at least. A period of two years was more usual; and the answer when it arrived might be merely a demand for more information. The delay was detrimental to efficient administration.

A system of checks and balances, of report, counter-report and comment, certainly ensured that all concerned obtained a hearing and that government was fully informed. But of equal certainty, the system impaired administrative efficiency, encouraged endless argument and led to indecision and delay.

In Spanish America there was no jurisdiction which could not be questioned and no decision that could not be reversed. Viceroys and

Captains-General were subject to the detailed and voluminous instructions they received from the Council of the Indies. Although theoretically they had the widest powers, in practice their hands were tied by the overriding authority of the council whose orders they had to follow. Projects they initiated had to be referred back to Spain for the approval of the Council.

Even when the Spanish Government had decided and had given firm instruction, appeals and counter-appeals might hold up essential action for years until the occasion for it was forgotten.

The emphasis on the appointment of continental Spaniards or 'peninsulares' in preference to colonial Spaniards or 'creoles' to important colonial offices, aroused the antagonism of the latter and resulted eventually in revolution against Spain and independence for the Spanish colonies in the early 19th century.

The Spanish system of colonial government had its defects; nevertheless, its achievements were impressive. The system was instrumental in creating orderly and prosperous colonies. The Crown was loyally served by its lawyer-officials as it was by its soldiers and priests. A great body of statute law was enacted, governing the relations between conquerors and conquered, and asserting the authority of the Crown and royal courts over all of them. Much of the legislation passed was a model of enlightenment for its time. The generous provision of courts, staffed by salaried professional judges who might be expected to be reasonably impartial, ensured that royal decrees were more than mere pious exhortations. Spanish imperial government was paternal, conscientious and legalistic. It was no more oppressive nor more corrupt than most contemporary European colonial governments. In some respects, at least in intention, it was markedly humane. Its achievements were to prove remarkably enduring.

3. British Colonial Government under the Lords-Proprietors

The degree of interest shown by European nations in their colonies was determined by the amount of wealth to be obtained from them. Though the British West Indian islands were claimed and settled in the name of the Crown, at first the English King made little attempt to exercise any control. The amount of wealth to be derived was small compared with the expense of colonising them. The King could ill-afford the cost involved in establishing settlements. The result was that he granted the islands to chosen noblemen—his favourites—who were given the title of Lords-Proprietors. For example, in 1627, the Earl of Carlisle was made Lord-Proprietor of the Leeward Caribbean Islands which were in process of being colonised. The grant was renewed in 1628 and Carlisle held the position until he died a bankrupt in 1636.

Although the Crown granted proprietary rights to the Lord-Proprietor, it did not allow the Lord-Proprietor to own the islands. These islands continued to exist as Crown domains. The Crown also reserved the right to determine who the Lord-Proprietor would be, to change him if necessary, to transfer the islands back under its own control, to delegate powers to the Lord-Proprietor, and to pass regulations governing the islands especially in the sphere of trade and the adjustment of duties. Effective control, however, at first rested with the Lord-Proprietor.

The powers of the Lord-Proprietor were wide. For instance, he could make laws for the colonies with the consent of the majority of the free-holders, he could erect courts and appoint judges, he could impose corporal punishment or the death sentence, and he could confer honours. He was responsible for the defence of the islands. Moreover, he had the right to tax the colonies and raise duties on their produce.

In return for his taxation of the colonists, the Lord-Proprietor was responsible for providing certain services for them. To the separate islands he appointed governors, tax-collectors, clergy and other officials through whom orderly administration could be conducted. He expended certain sums of money upon guns, munitions and the erection of fortifications. In addition, he maintained the only real liaison between the settlements and the English Government.

For the most part, the Lord-Proprietor resided in England. His place in each colony was taken by a governor whom he appointed and commissioned to exercise his extensive powers. In order to assist him, the governor appointed a council, taking care to choose men who would support him effectively. The members of the council were selected from among the leading and most influential planters. Beginning in 1639 in Barbados, an assembly was also formed in each colony. Its members were elected by free-holders from among the planters to assist the governor and council. The governors and councils were the only executive, judicial and legislative authority in the colonies before the creation of assemblies. When assemblies were formed, they assisted in the legislation of laws.

Many of the proceedings of the legislative system were unpopular, and since the authorities had no independent military force at their disposal, the success of their administration depended on their personal ability and mastery of men.

The authorities naturally took advantage of their power to push their own fortunes and the resultant state of affairs was that a large and discontented majority paid sullen obedience to a small ruling clique ever on the watch to anticipate resistance and dealt with by harsh measures.

4. The Old Representative System

The proprietary system of colonial government was replaced from around 1660 by the Old Representative System. The system was changed in order to permit more direct participation by the British Government. By that time the royal domains were being enlarged. For instance, Jamaica had been acquired in 1655 and more and more lands in America and the West Indies were being colonised. Colonial government was in urgent need of overhaul. Colonies were becoming increasingly prosperous since the cultivation of sugar-cane was introduced around 1640 and promised large revenues to the Crown. Direct control of colonial government was in keeping with the policy of centralisation evident since 1650 with the passing of a Navigation Act. Shortly after 1660 the King prepared to resume possession of the Caribbean islands from the Lords-Proprietors. The system of government which emerged in the colonies bore a close resemblance to the British system. Thus there was a governor representing the King, a council corresponding to the House of Lords and an assembly corresponding to the House of Commons.

A colonial governor was charged with the preservation of the royal prerogative and was given appropriate powers. He had power to select a council to assist him, to convoke, adjourn and dissolve the legislature, and to approve or veto legislation. He had the right to establish courts and to appoint judges, magistrates and Justices of the Peace. In addition, he could pardon criminal offenders. The governor was the only person who could dispose of offices and establish fees for them. He was the Commander-in-Chief of all military forces; he was authorised to organise a militia, to raise appropriate defences and to deal with local insurrection and foreign invasion. He was empowered to regulate commerce, to establish markets and fairs, to set up havens and ports, and to grant charters of incorporation to deserving bodies. Finally, the governor had power to grant licences of marriage, letters of administration and probate of wills, and to make appointments to all vacant benefices.

While the governor had extensive powers, the freedom with which he exercised those powers was limited. From the very first, the consent of the local council was necessary for him to perform his duties. The members of the council were nominated by the governor and approved by the Crown. From the earliest years, the council consisted of twelve members, and after some fluctuations, from 1697 onwards it was fixed at that number. The council was presided over by a president who was its most senior member, and it performed a dual function: in the transaction of administrative business it was an advisory body to the governor; and in law-making sessions, it was a true legislative council, the upper house of the legislature. As befitted its status, the council was naturally invested with a good deal of dignity as well as authority. It had as its clerk and marshal the deputy-secretary and deputy-provost marshal of the colony, and it gradually developed its own code of rules and privileges.

The assembly was elected from among white adults who satisfied certain property qualifications. Electors were white adult freeholders and owners of a certain amount of property. Slaves and free negroes and coloured people did not have the vote and could not stand for elections, in the case of slaves throughout slavery and in the case of free negroes and coloureds until the early years of the 19th century. The assembly was the lower house of the legislature. The number of members was not fixed but varied from island to island. The assembly met under the chairmanship of its own speaker. It drew up its own rules of conduct, disciplined its members, judged of their qualifications, and decided all disputed elections. In addition, it could enquire into public grievances, summon persons before it, commit for contempt, and even 'impeach' high public dignitaries for gross misdemeanours. The privileges of assemblymen included freedom of speech and debate and extended even to immunity from personal arrest during the entire period of each assembly.

Laws in each colony were usually enacted by the governor, council and assembly. Having passed each House three times, they were presented to the governor for his assent which was normally given provided the laws did not infringe the terms of his Commission and Instructions. The Acts then went into operation. In the case of ordinary bills, it did not matter into which House they were first introduced, but Money Bills were customarily introduced in the assembly which claimed the sole right to initiate taxation and manage the colony's revenue. After an Act had received the governor's assent, it was sent to England to receive royal approval. The Crown, through the Secretary of State for the Colonies, could exercise the power of confirmation, disallowance or suspension. If approved, the Act remained in operation, but it went out of operation if suspended or disallowed. Some Acts were merely allowed to 'lie by', that is, they were kept in operation for an indefinite period, since they could be disallowed at any time. However, this led to uncertainty about their authority in the colonies.

Though resembling the parent body, colonial legislatures were subordinate to it in all important respects. Their laws were subject to disallowance if found to conflict with English law or policy. The islands were subject to imperial legislation, even taxation, when an English Act included them. The legislatures could not deal with foreign affairs. The governors and chief office-holders within the islands were appointed under letters-patent by the Crown itself, indicating clearly that the island administrations were considered an integral part of the royal jurisdiction. Island legislatures had unfettered right to make whatever laws they chose provided they were not repugnant to the laws of Britain or unduly restrictive of the royal prerogative. But at the same time they were far from being independent.

5. The reasons for conflict between British West Indian Assemblies and the Colonial Office in the 18th century

Conflicts between the British West Indian Assemblies and the Colonial Office were inevitable in a system of colonial government which gave to colonial legislatures the assumptions of responsibility but which withheld real power from them. Also, much of the trouble arose because the legislatures asserted power which they believed to be rightfully theirs. The problem was complicated by the unique economic and social organisation of the British West Indies.

Theoretically, British West Indian legislatures were supreme in the law-making process but in practice all laws passed had to be approved by the imperial government which, in turn, could enact legislation to govern the colonies. This arrangement led to a double conflict. In the first place, laws were sometimes passed by the colonial legislatures which were not approved by the Colonial Office, the administrative department of the British Government. On the other hand, West Indian legislatures objected to imperial legislation as being incompatible with their sovereign rights. The fact that imperial enactments usually had great permanence, in addition to the fact that West Indian legislatures could argue greater or fuller knowledge of, and acquaintance with, local problems led the latter bodies to claim a more decisive voice in decision making.

West Indians writhed under some of the imperial regulations which limited their freedom of action. Among these were the Navigation Laws which confined the major part of the colonial trade to Britain and excluded direct trade with continental Europe and at times with the United States. The restriction was more irksome when there was local distress due to inadequacy of supplies or when foreign trade could have been more profitable than the British. Planters in the colonies were anxious to secure personal fortunes so that they could return to England. Insofar as these planters were members of the local legislatures and insofar as the British Government through the Colonial Office limited their profits and thwarted their ambitions by means of restrictive legislation, the stage was set for friction in the assemblies.

Two other features of colonial administration explain the causes of conflict. The first was England's obligation to defend the colonies against enemy attack; and the second was the final control which the legislatures possessed in the disbursement of public funds. When the colonists suspected Britain of a denial of responsibility for defence, they retaliated by withholding essential supplies of money to pay Crown officials employed in the colonies and to whose maintenance they contributed.

Local legislative control over money was used in another way to frustrate the intentions of the Colonial Office. Colonial Assemblies in particular often claimed more privileges than those to which they were entitled. In most of the colonies, the assemblies made themselves the predominant partner in government and claimed the sole right to initiate Money Bills. These bills were often used to introduce controversial legislation, that is, legislation which might be contrary to the policies of the Colonial Office. The method adopted was to tack these on to Money Bills with the clear understanding that if the Colonial Office wanted money it had to approve of the measures tacked on to the bill.

The sanctity of private property was recognised as one of the basic rights of Englishmen under the law, and Englishmen abroad asserted and claimed the same rights as Englishmen at home. At the same time, one of the essential features of West Indian society before 1834 was the existence of slavery. Slavery was a subject for continuous dispute between the colonies and the metropolis since the colonists objected to any interference by the British Government in any matter which pertained to their property in slaves. The debates over the abolition of the slave trade, the amelioration of the conditions under which slaves lived and worked, and the emancipation of slaves, bear ample testimony to this.

It is necessary to remember that the geographical separation of the Colonial Office from the West Indies made the governor, as representative of the Crown, the butt of antagonism and opposition towards the British Government by the legislatures. This method of attack was effective since the governor, despite his clearly defined instructions from London, was in a vulnerable position since planters could use their influence in London to secure the recall of a governor who was not amenable to local demands. In any case, many governors lacked the patience, the local knowledge and political acumen to resist. They were susceptible to pressure.

6. The introduction of Crown Colony Government

With the continuing decline of British West Indian plantocracy after 1838, and the emancipation of slaves, the British Government was faced with two alternatives as far as the system of colonial government was concerned. It could have retained the old representative system of government with an extension of the franchise to include the ex-slaves, or it could abrogate all existing political rights and assume direct and full responsibility for the administration of the colonies. Several factors were responsible for the adoption of the second alternative by which Crown Colony Government was introduced in the West Indian colonies.

(i) British West Indian Assemblies which were elected were based on a severely limited franchise; at best, they represented only the planter, merchant and legal classes.

(ii) The assemblies were the tools of the creole ruling classes and they were used as such. They were reactionary on every important West Indian issue and had shown their unwillingness to introduce progressive measures about such matters as slavery, emancipation, religious toleration and economic improvement. Their attitudes did not change after 1838.

(iii) It could perhaps be argued that in a legal sense colonies were communities of white emigrant settlers and that the assemblies were more or less representative bodies. But emancipation, by which slaves acquired the status of colonists also, robbed this argument of any validity and made the old constitutional system obsolete and undesirable.

(iv) The system which the British Government intended to introduce was already being practised in British Guiana, St. Lucia and Trinidad, where it had proved successful in enabling the British Government to introduce measures unpopular with the ruling classes.

(v) The bankruptcy of ideas of the ruling classes was matched by a similar bankruptcy of ideas among the governors whom they attacked as enemies of the liberties of the white British West Indians.

(vi) The choice of Crown Colony Government stemmed also from the fear of the masses. The idea that agricultural labourers, and negro at that, should be granted political power must have seemed the height of absurdity. Fear of the negro masses and the conviction that negroes could never look after themselves, lay at the heart of British policy.

(vii) The direct participation of the Crown in the governmental process in the West Indies was considered essential to hold the balance between continuing white oligarchic tyranny and the presumed democratic ineptitude, ignorance and inexperience of the negro.

(viii) The majority of the English educated class as well as the expatriate British officials in the colonies, believed as an article of faith in the cultural, sometimes in the racial inferiority of West Indians whether white or black.

(ix) In Colonial Office theory, West Indians were gradually being groomed for self-government; in preparation for this eventuality a period of training was essential.

7. Advantages of Crown Colony Government

(*a*) It allowed the Crown more extensive powers, and therefore more freedom of manoeuvre, than the assemblies had ever had. This meant that Crown Colony Government could function efficiently and without recourse to local interests even in emergency situations.

(*b*) Crown Colony Government was not wholly repressive.

(*c*) It was profoundly constitutionalist as can be judged by the strict adherence to constitutionalism by West Indians to-day.

(*d*) Crown Colony Government created no departures from the rule of law, even during the periods of greatest stress, to secure constitutional reform. There were occasional outbreaks of violence, but there was no national outbreak of terrorist activities designed to disrupt the whole system.

(*e*) The constitutional defect of the old representative system of government, namely, that it failed to provide a clear source of power for decision-taking and law-making, was settled. Under Crown Colony Government, the executive could by-pass legislative opposition. Power lay clearly at the centre.

(*f*) Governors, administrators and commissioners were still open to influence by responsible public opinion and in their exercise of a benevolent despotism they were not pure autocrats.

(*g*) The power of the governor to nominate non-officials to the legislative council enabled him to give a popular base to the government by appointing representatives from all important sections of the coimmunity.

(*h*) Despite its failures, Crown Colony Government exemplified British political tradition in colonial administration in its essential nature—incorruptible, motivated by high ideals, concerned for civil liberties and betraying a real passionate consciousness to duty and conduct.

8. Disadvantages of Crown Colony Government

(*a*) It perpetuated colonial subordination to an imperial power in greater measure since even existing representation was whittled away.

(*b*) A system in which the executive could ignore legislative opposition and in which the governor tended to appoint men from the dominant groups to the executive and legislative council was clearly undemocratic.

(*c*) Crown Colony Government emphasised the irresponsibility of the non-elected executive and legislative bodies and bred arrogance by officials towards nominated non-officials.

(*d*) In any conflict of interest the official view eventually prevailed by means of the governor's casting vote or by means of the use of the official majority.

(*e*) It robbed those who participated in it of self-respect since, for example, ex-officio members were bound to support a measure irrespective of their own views.

(*f*) Where elected members existed, Crown Colony Government was also morally disastrous since these members were forced into opposition, and given little opportunity to exercise responsibility.

(*g*) The key figure was the governor and the system depended for success on his ability. The recruitment of governors from the lesser ranks of scholarly English gentlemen into the overseas career service left much to be desired in terms of interest and ability to work the system.

(*h*) Crown Colony Government was not on the side of the ordinary people but continued to favour vested interests, invariably white. White colonists were usually supported by the governor and were the real makers of government policy. Where the association of non-whites was tolerated, it was because they shared the views of the white ruling class.

(*i*) Through the adoption of Crown Colony Government, the imperial power took control of constitutional change and development in the British West Indies. But the slowness with which it moved forced educated and other interested West Indians to seek constitutional reform through their own efforts and initiative. After the social disturbances of the 1930's, Britain was forced to concede the need for change.

(*j*) Crown Colony Government did not lead to the notable social and economic changes which it was expected to produce. The administrative officers recruited in England exhibited little initiative in introducing improved measures of social and economic reform.

9. The Morant Bay Uprising and Crown Colony Government in Jamaica, 1865–1866

The transformation of the old representative system to Crown Colony Government can best be seen in Jamaica, which was in the mid-19th century the most important British colony in the West Indies. The working of the old representative system of government in Jamaica showed all of the basic weaknesses of that system, only in this case, because of the greater size of Jamaica compared with the rest of the British West Indies, on a larger scale. The system was brought to an abrupt end as a result of the revolt by peasants at Morant Bay in St. Thomas in the east of the island. In itself, the Morant Bay Uprising was comparatively unimportant, but it led to a virtual political revolution in Jamaica when the obsolete, decrepit and reactionary system of government was swept away to be replaced by a more workable one. The movement which started in Jamaica eventually led to similar reform in other British West Indian colonies.

The Morant Bay Uprising had its origin in increasing social tensions and economic hardships since full emancipation in 1838. The following factors were important:

(i) The period after 1838 was one of worsening relations between planter-employers and negro-employees. Emancipation converted slaves into free people who could decide how they would be employed in future and for whom. To the anger of planters and their sympathisers, many ex-slaves preferred to work for themselves on their own plots away from the estates. Many of these people were stigmatised as being lazy. For those who remained on the estates, their treatment hardly improved beyond the conditions which prevailed during slavery, since employers had not learnt better ways of treating their employees.

(ii) Between 1838 and 1865, economic conditions in Jamaica fluctuated, and in 1865 they were very bad. Between 1855 and 1860, sugar prices were better than they had been for many years, but between 1860 and 1861 prices fell from 26/10 to 23/5 a cwt. and continued low during the American Civil War (1861–1865) when sugar hitherto sent to America was diverted to England instead. Because of the dominance of sugar, the slump in prices affected other aspects of the economy.

(iii) Lower prices for sugar led planters to give lower wages or to require more work for the same money paid. At the same time, because of the American Civil War, the prices of imported food-stuffs were increasing. The effect on the labouring class was severe.

(iv) A religious revival among the peasants after 1860 led to their temporary desertion of farmlands, so that at the time of low wages and dear imports, local produce was scarce on the market.

(v) Because of the negro drift away from the estates, the planters resorted to the immigration of Indian indentures in order to provide the estates with sufficient labourers. This reduced the number of estate jobs available to negroes, and those who had left the estates could not readily find employment during the depression.

(vi) To add to the general distress, in May and June, 1864, floods created widespread damage to food-crops. Droughts which followed retarded production. The prices of provisions increased almost everywhere in Jamaica.

(vii) Appeals to the British Government for the adoption of appropriate measures to alleviate the distress of the people—a letter from E. B. Underhill, secretary of the Baptist Missionary Society, and a petition from the people of St. Ann—produced no satisfactory response. Indeed, 'The Queen's Advice' in reply to the St. Ann petition, urged the people to seek 'their advancement through their own merits and efforts'.

(viii) Mass meetings were held throughout Jamaica in 1865 at which Governor Eyre and the colonial legislature were urged to take some action to relieve the distress. The requests fell on deaf ears, and the people no doubt came to believe that they should indeed seek 'their advancement through their own . . . efforts'.

The scene for the Morant Bay Uprising was set in St. Thomas in the east. St. Thomas was administered by a Custos, Baron von Ketelhodt, and Vestry who were not only corrupt and inefficient but unpopular since they were partly responsible for the dismissal of a local idol, George William Gordon, from the Commission of the Peace. Against the Custos and Vestry, the pent-up social and economic grievances of the people found full expression.

Between the 7th and 9th of October, 1865, Paul Bogle, a local leader, and his associates, were responsible for disturbing a number of court cases. They were ordered to be arrested, but when the police tried to carry out the order, they were beaten. In the face of threats,

the local militia was called out and Governor Eyre despatched troops
to the area in response to requests for military assistance. Martial law
was declared. The people stormed and set fire to the courthouse and
then proceeded to plunder the neighbouring sugar estates. In all, the
rioters killed twenty-two people, including the Custos, and wounded
about thirty-four others; they plundered twenty houses and shops and
burnt five buildings including the courthouse. Such destruction was
followed by swift retribution. The toll taken by the armed forces in the
initial stages of the riot is unknown, but later 439 rioters were executed,
including Gordon and Bogle, 600 were flogged and nearly a thousand
peasant houses destroyed.

The uprising was confined to St. Thomas, probably because of
the swift action taken, but it frightened the authorities. The opportunity was seized by Governor Eyre to effect the constitutional reform
he had long desired, namely, the abolition of the local assembly.
It was a peculiarity of the colonial political system that, barring an
Act of British Parliament, reform of the legislature could only be
effected by the colonial legislature itself. Presenting the picture of
violence and death at the hands of vengeful negroes, Eyre succeeded in
getting the assembly to join in passing an Act for its own abolition.
The Act introduced a single-chambered legislative council in place
of the council and assembly, half of its members to be elected and half
nominated. In such a body the Governor was almost sure of carrying
measures he supported with the help of the nominated members.

With the adoption and implementation of this Act, Crown Colony
Government was instituted in Jamaica in 1866. From there the system
was gradually extended to other British West Indian colonies—for
example, to the British Virgin Islands in 1867, to Antigua and Grenada
in 1898, and to British Guiana in 1928. Of the British West Indian
colonies, only Barbados remained outside the pale of Crown Colony
Government.

10. Government of the French West Indies

When Cardinal Richelieu came to power in France in 1623, his aim
was to make France a great power in Europe. One way was to break
Spanish power in America and to this end he encouraged the establishment of settlements. French merchants were not anxious to raise
capital for settlements and in order to support individual efforts such as
those of D'Esnambuc in St. Christopher and of L'Olive and Duplessis in
Guadeloupe and Martinique, Richelieu promoted joint stock companies such as the Company of St. Christopher and the Company of
the Isles of America. Richelieu appointed the directors of both companies and empowered them to control colonial affairs.

In the West Indies, the men responsible for settling the colonies were made Governors—D'Esnambuc in St. Christopher, L'Olive in Guadeloupe and Duplessis in Martinique. In 1635 when the last two islands were colonised, D'Esnambuc was appointed Governor-General by Richelieu.

It does not appear that the directors were effective in giving direction to the young colonies, and it was left largely to the Governor-General (at first D'Esnambuc, and then De Poincy after him) to make the decisions necessary for the development of the colonies. They were independent and often arbitrary in their methods, and because each governor was anxious to develop his colony in his own way, often in competition with the others, dissention was bound to occur between them and the Governor-General. On one occasion, de Poincy went to the extent of imprisoning L'Olive.

In 1645 the power of the governors was strengthened when they were authorised to try law cases locally instead of sending them to France. For this purpose the governor and the members of the council whom he nominated, were made supreme judges in their own island. Most of these cases involved disputes between planters over lands. Occasionally, the affairs of the colonies were investigated by individual directors of the company or by royal officials.

In 1648, French colonial governors reached the height of their independence and power when the Company of the Isles of America became bankrupt. The islands were sold to the men who were governors at the time: De Poincy in St. Christopher, Houel in Guadeloupe and du Parquet in Martinique. They were little more than despots.

The proprietorship system of colonial government continued in the French colonies until 1664 when Colbert, the great French Minister of Finance, made arrangements for resumption of control by the French Government. Again, however, the administration of the colonies was entrusted to a new Company, called the Compagnie des Indes Occidentales. This Company also became bankrupt and was terminated in 1674.

After 1674 the Crown assumed direct control, and the colonies were governed by a dual administration. Supreme command was given to a Governor-General, and under him were the military governors of the several islands. In addition, each island had a civil administrator, or intendant, who was chiefly responsible for justice, economic affairs and finance. Each governor was also assisted by a council of about ten members who advised him on matters of policy. The council was nominated by the governor, and its president was the intendant.

The French colonial governors had considerable powers, notably in matters of defence, and in this respect they could make demands on the colonists to use their slaves for constructing fortifications and other public works. Much of their success, however, depended on the support they received from their councils. The councils neither voted money nor made laws since taxation and legislation were both done by royal decree. But members of the council were prominent people and wielded considerable influence. They tended to claim rights similar to those exercised by the French 'parlements', just as the British colonial assemblies claimed rights similar to those of the House of Commons.

French colonial administration was centralised in France since the local councils were advisory bodies and did not have powers of legislation. A change was made in 1787 when assemblies were introduced in the colonies, and early in the French Revolution, the colonies secured representation in the French National Assembly. After 1815, when the Bourbon monarchy was restored in France, both systems were abolished—the colonists ceased to legislate for themselves or to influence French opinion in 'parlement'. By this time, St. Domingue had declared its independence as Haiti.

In 1831 full civil rights were granted to free coloured people in the French colonies. In 1834 colonial councils were created in Martinique and Guadeloupe, the members of which were elected on a very restricted franchise. The powers of the councils to legislate were very limited and all laws could be overridden by the French National Assembly.

After the 1848 Revolution in France the colonies were once again given direct representation in France on a greatly enlarged franchise. Each island was given three representatives. This privilege was suspended in 1854 but was restored in 1871. Representatives included both white and (more numerous) coloured persons.

After 1848 French colonial politics were marked by a shift in the balance of political power from the whites to the coloureds and in the integration of colonies more closely with France rather than in decentralisation of power and independence.

Conclusion

The Spanish system of colonial government was designed to strengthen royal control over its colonial empire. It was centralised in Spain in the Council of the Indies and the House of Trade. In the colonies, there were the viceroys, the audiencias, and the provincial governors, all of whom were peninsular Spaniards. Only cabildos were colonial Spaniards and their powers were relatively small. To check on its colonial officials, the Crown instituted the 'visita' and the 'residencia'. The system suffered from over-centralisation which resulted in delayed action, and it bred hostility between 'peninsulares' and 'creoles'.

However, a lot of good was still achieved, and many of the achievements were lasting. The system was no more oppressive than those of the other European nations.

In contrast to the Spanish system, the English and French systems of colonial government were more decentralised. In the British system, for example, after control was taken from the Lords-Proprietors, the British Government directed colonial affairs through a particular council in England, and governors in the colonies. A large measure of control over their own affairs was given to the colonists through representative assemblies. The British Government retained control over foreign affairs and trade, and reserved the right to legislate for the colonies and to sanction the laws which the colonists had passed. These restrictions often resulted in conflict between the colonial assemblies and the British Government. Besides, the political powers given to the colonists often enabled them to flout the expressed desires of the British Government, especially since colonists claimed the same rights and privileges as Englishmen in Britain. The refusal of assemblies to adopt the amelioration proposals suggested by the British Government in the 1820's led the latter to conclude on the desirability of reform. After the full emancipation of slaves in 1838, the representative system gradually gave way to the Crown Colony system of colonial government.

The differences in organisation and function between Spanish colonial government and that of the British West Indies, were also observed in the case of the religious denominations which constituted another important part of colonial society.

Revision Questions

1. In what ways can it be said that Spanish colonial government was highly centralised?
2. How did Spain seek to control the political and economic affairs of its colonies?
3. What was there in Spanish colonial government to condemn and praise?
4. Why did the English have proprietary colonies? What were their chief features?
5. Compare the English and French systems of colonial government in the 18th century. Was reform of these systems needed?
6. Why was there friction between British West Indian Assemblies and British colonial governors?

6. The Religious Denominations

The various religious denominations active in the West Indian colonies reflected the denominational diversity existing in the European colonising powers. Ecclesiastical activities were generally encouraged (in different degrees in different colonies) as a 'civilising' influence: the churches wished to convert to Christianity (and 'civilised' ways) the native Indians and the new negro workers alike. But there were important differences of attitude in the different colonies.

The Spanish colonial empire was served exclusively by the clergy of the Roman Catholic Church which received active government support and encouragement. This support recognised the fact that the Spanish Church was an essential instrument of government and empire-building.

In the British colonies, preference was given to the Anglican Church as the established church of the colonising power, but Anglicanism was not sponsored in the same way as the Spanish Church. And other non-Catholic denominations were tolerated. The main duties of the Anglican Church and of the non-conformist missions which soon sprang up were pastoral and not political. The Anglican preference was evident mainly from the additional obstacles placed by the colonists around the activities of the missions.

The French colonies resembled the British in their attitude to religion. The Catholic Church was preferred, but it was not the sole denomination allowed to function in the French colonies.

The English and French colonists were not particularly noted for their religious inclinations, and their hostile attitude accounted for the many obstacles which they placed in the way of the clergy and missionaries who sought to cultivate their religious views. Wherever the work of the missions was tolerated, if not actively encouraged, it was because slave-owners recognised the benefits of religion in making their slaves easier to control and more willing to undertake the arduous work of plantation agriculture. Generally, opposition to the religious activities of the clergy and missionaries was strongest in the hey-day of sugar production. The situation changed somewhat in the 19th century with the depression in the sugar industry and with the abolition of the slave trade. In the British colonies, the illegality of importing fresh supplies of slaves to replace those who had been lost forced slave-owners to give more humane treatment to those who remained in order to secure their maximum performance. The clergy and missionaries were used as the instruments of the policy of voluntary amelioration. Some colonies went to the extent of voting supplies of money for the incumbent of the Anglican Church in order to secure his fullest co-operation in regulating the social system.

The greater accommodation given to the missions was reflected in the greater scope of their work. From being primarily concerned with conversions and baptisms, and with officiating at weddings and funerals, their functions extended to such public services as the establishment of schools for the provision of education and to the dispensation of poor relief. Considering the difficulties, physical, financial and otherwise which they suffered, this further recognition of their presence in society undoubtedly gave personal satisfaction and moral encouragement to the clergy and missionaries.

1. The role of the Church in the Spanish American Empire

The first priest to the New World is supposed to have accompanied Christopher Columbus on his second voyage. Since then the Spanish Crown generally followed the principle of having a bishopric established immediately after a new region was colonised. The most numerous clergy in the Indies at the beginning were the friars who came out at an early date. After a time they were replaced by secular priests.

A number of factors governed the role of the Church in Spanish America. Since the dominant note of Spanish society during and after the period of discovery was religion, it is not surprising that the Church should play a leading part in the Empire. This was especially so since in matters pertaining to doctrine and religion, the Church in America was under the direct control of the Crown in whose name the new lands were discovered. In fact, in a very real sense, the Church was just another branch of royal government and another means of political control over the colonists. The Church was noted for its strong royalism and through spiritual and moral influence maintained royal dominion over the growing American Empire. It was largely through the Church that Spain succeeded in transmitting its culture and political ascendancy.

Acting in conjunction with the conquistadores or military explorers, the Church was a vital part of the Spanish system of colonisation and one of the most outstanding pioneering devices of the Spanish Government. By its discipline and by the methods it adopted, the Church was almost a military and political agency designed to push forward and defend the colonial frontiers, pacify the natives and open the way to European occupation. The subjection of the native Indians and the extension of the territorial boundaries emphasised the role of the Church. Its function was to 'civilise' the savage frontier and to press it further inland away from established European centres in order to further colonisation. The Church also served to maintain colonial borders against foreign encroachment. One vehicle by which it sought to do this was the Inquisition. By its exclusion of heretical Protestants and by its strict censorship of books, the Church made foreign political and philosophical ideas difficult or dangerous to obtain and served as a defensive mechanism of the Empire.

The Church was not only an advance post of empire and a political device of colonialism. It had its own religious objectives and interests. Priests were chiefly concerned with superintending the work of converting the 'primitive' natives to Christianity and protecting them from exploitation. The earliest and most energetic group were the friars, of whom the Dominicans were prominent. Later, the Franciscans and Jesuits became more active.

Associated with their attention to the spiritual needs of conversion, the priests endeavoured to eliminate 'heathen' practices among those baptised. Native temples were everywhere torn down and idols burnt or smashed. It does not appear, however, that there was any wholesale destruction of manuscripts and picture-writings of the Indians.

Priests were also concerned with the material and physical welfare of the natives. They considered the care of the sick and needy in hospitals and almshouses an essential part of their mission. Hospitals were particularly needed because of the terrible epidemics which occasionally swept the land. A hospital not only provided treatment for the sick, but was frequently a kind of poor-house as well, where the aged and infirm could be attended to, and where poor-relief could be dispensed. Virtually all the social services in the Spanish colonies were provided by the clergy. In addition to hospitals, they constructed and managed asylums and schools. Schools were attached to monasteries, and local colleges and universities were staffed by priests who were able thereby to influence people's thoughts.

It was among the natives that the clergy showed the greatest energy and zeal. They traversed deserts and forests, studied native languages and customs, and endured great hardships, hunger, pests and diseases. In order to introduce the elements of European culture most effectively, the priests gathered the natives into villages or missions and gave instruction in agriculture and industry, handicrafts, arts and letters.

Explorations by missionary priests extended the contemporary knowledge of geography, botany and zoology, as well as providing invaluable information on aboriginal languages and customs. Despite the handicaps imposed by climate and geography, some of the missions became quite productive following the establishment of cattle-ranches and sugar plantations. Cotton cloth, hammocks and leather goods were produced, and fruit culture, tobacco and cocoa cultivation were promoted.

In Spanish America there was little surplus capital and little banking. When an improvident landowner needed capital he applied to the monasteries. Because of their profitable activities and thrift, these were able to accumulate capital for investment.

However, despite the advances achieved in creating some prosperity and in saving the Indians from exploitation, the work of the Church often caused distress and was sometimes harmful.

The genuineness of Indian conversion is doubtful. Evidence shows that under the cloak of Christian rites many Indians retained their old beliefs. With regard to conversion, also, not all of the clergy proved themselves worthy of their high calling and many natives were often accepted into the Church without sufficient instruction or preparation. Baptised Indians were often severely punished physically in order to abolish their 'heathen' practices. The Indians had been conquered not only militarily but also spiritually as well. Their traditional religious life was suppressed and their gods destroyed. Their social customs were disorganised and disrupted and their priests and leaders often killed.

Monasteries grew in wealth and numbers beyond the needs and conditions of a pioneer settlement. The erection and upkeep of churches and monasteries and the maintenance of a numerous clergy were accomplished through the forced labour of the Indians under the repartimiento system and this increased their burdens and added to their humiliation.

The ecclesiastical establishment was an economic burden on the colonies. The acquisition of much of the best land by way of benefactions, purchase or mortgage discouraged immigration and did not lead to the economic or profitable use of the soil. Ecclesiastical taxation, particularly the tithe, was prejudicial to the progress and prosperity of a young, frontier, agricultural society.

2. Functions of the clergy and missionaries in the British Colonies

Except for the appointment of an occasional catechist to conduct divine service and to give religious instruction to slaves, no systematic attempt was made to introduce a vital religious system in the West Indies until the second half of the 18th century. During and after that time there was a strong growth of religious effort by Anglicans, Moravians and Methodists, to name only the most active Christian denominations operating in the West Indies.

Until the end of the 18th century and, in certain cases, for some time after that, the activities of the Anglican clergy were more or less confined to the minority of white colonists to whom they were closely associated by family connections and interests. The attention of the other denominations were primarily devoted to the negro and coloured population.

The white inhabitants of the West Indies did not see much virtue in accepting the Christian religion for its own sake. Insofar as they tolerated the efforts of the missionaries and clergy, it was because they recognised the efficacy of religion in making their slaves more tractable and consequently more valuable as plantation labourers.

In keeping with their close association with the whites, the clergy performed unique functions. For example, they took part as ex-officio members in the conduct of local government, and some of them held civil and political offices. Clergymen served as members of the colonial legislatures, and occupied seats both in the council and assembly.

In addition, as members of the state church, the clergy assisted in the dispensation of social services. In the colonial society, during slavery, there was no separate organisation for the distribution of, say, poor relief. This work was done by the local vestries under the control of the clergy.

Apart from these two functions which were performed by the clergy, the roles of the missionaries and the Anglican clergy had certain similarities:

(i) The duty of conversion. For this purpose chapels and churches were established in which instruction and sermons were delivered. The business of conversion was the most important. As one missionary put it, 'The love of souls surmounts every difficulty'. With varying degrees of emphasis, the clergy and missionaries attended to both whites and negroes, free and slave. Their achievements were remarkable. By 1800, in the Leeward Islands alone, out of a total population of about 83,000 negroes and coloureds, the missionaries had converted as many as 23,700.

(ii) They attended to duties of baptism associated with conversion, and of marriage and death.

(iii) They established Sunday schools and, later, day schools, as far as their finances permitted or the attitude of planters allowed. There they taught religious knowledge, and the rudiments of reading, writing and arithmetic.

In order to facilitate the process of instruction and conversion, the Moravians, for instance, not only learnt the languages of the negroes but translated relevant parts of the Bible into creole and other languages.

Through their functions of instruction and conversion, the Chapel and Church provided the opportunity for the negro population to obtain training in responsibility and leadership by enabling them to supervise the education of converts and to assist in the Sunday schools. After a time, most of the day-school teachers were coloured women and the catechists were coloured men.

By insisting on adherence by the converts to the Christian precepts of virtue and morality, the clergy and missionaries aided the negro converts in throwing off their African culture and in adhering to the patterns of western behaviour exhibited by the white population. One example of the change was the substitution of the African polygamous marriage for the European monogamous marriage. The work of the denominations, therefore, introduced new values into the ranks of the slaves and promoted cultural assimilation.

The denominations sometimes attended to more secular matters. For example, in Antigua the missionaries were successful in forming in 1793 and 1794 a corps of militia from among their converts to assist in the defence of the island.

The denominations sought the co-operation of the colonial whites in order to promote their job of conversion, and so did not directly attack the social order. Rather, insofar as they preached obedience and subordination to the negroes, they sought to maintain that order. Nevertheless, because the slave-owners needed the support and co-operation of the denominations to preserve order among the slaves after 1808 when the slave trade was abolished, they were forced to modify their attitudes and behave in a manner more in conformity with the teachings of the denominations. Negro conditions became somewhat alleviated.

The activities of the denominations were of great benefit to the whites. By inculcating a sense of moral obligation in the slaves, they sought to promote the subordination of the slaves in the society. By giving a religious bias to education, by preaching the virtues of industry, honesty and obedience, and by keeping the standard of education low, the denominations sought to make the slaves better labourers and at the same time unable to contemplate more worth-while alternatives than plantation labour.

But by their devotion to the negro population and by the services they rendered, the denominations became one of the most potent social forces in the West Indies. Through their activities especially, the slaves were introduced to the world of knowledge beyond the confines of the estates. Advantage was taken of this knowledge by the negroes, after full emancipation, to work out a destiny divorced from plantation agriculture.

3. Attitude of the planters towards the Anglican clergy in British Colonies

There was strong anti-Roman Catholicism in the British colonies. As a result, the clergy of the Roman Catholic Church were not toler-ated. In this respect the colonists followed the example of contemporary trends in England. In contrast, preference was given to the clergy of the Anglican Church since Anglicanism was the established religion in England. Though not strongly religious themselves, the whites nevertheless sought to maintain the trappings of a sophisticated English society. Priests were required to perform the rituals of baptism, marriage and burial. In time, other benefits and privileges were exten-ded to the Church. The favourable attitude of planters towards the clergy may be summarised as follows:

 (i) Before 1800 preachers were permitted to take out licences but they were not allowed to instruct slaves or to open schools.

 (ii) The sacraments and sacramental offices of the Church were provided for the whites and freeman and scales of fee were fixed by law.

 (iii) The clergy kept registers of baptisms, marriages and deaths, and these registers had official validity.

 (iv) The Houses of the Legislature had their chaplains and for years the meetings of the legislature were held in churches. Here, also, elections took place.

 (v) The clergy were ex-officio members of the assemblies and in some colonies were the chairmen.

 (vi) The provision for the support of the Clergy came partly from the colonial Treasuries, partly from fees for services performed, and partly from vestry allowances. Incomes varied greatly from time to time and between individuals, but were generally on a liberal scale. Legislatures were always generous in their financial treatment of the Clergy.

The favourable response of the whites to the activities of the Clergy was not universal or widespread. Many parishes were without clergy and churches because the white residents withheld their support. In Tobago until 1812, for example, there were seven parishes with only one clergyman and no church. Generally, churches were small and within the reach of few people except those in the towns. They were thinly attended except at funerals or on special occasions. Baptisms and marriages were performed in houses. Where there was no incumbent, Churchwardens and Justices of the Peace officiated.

Generally speaking, the white colonists were not religious. In so far as they encouraged religious activities among the slaves, it was because they recognised the value of religion in making the slaves more docile, more manageable, less likely to rebel against authority, and more willing to work. Especially in the 18th century, planters tended to resist any attempts to educate slaves. Co-operation between planters and the Clergy, however, increased in the 19th century prior to emancipation, when planters saw the necessity of using the influence of the Clergy to make slaves perform at their best.

4. Attitude of the planters towards the missionaries in British Colonies

In contrast to the attitude of the whites towards the Anglican Clergy, their attitude towards the missionaries, primarily Wesleyan Methodists and Moravians, was one of more or less decided opposition. There were only rare exceptions. The missionaries began evangelising in the West Indies in the latter half of the 18th century. At first there was limited acquiescence by the planters to the missionaries' activities, but gradually opposition began to increase.

When the slave trade and the system of slavery itself became subjects of hot political discussion in England in the late 18th and early 19th centuries, the missionaries were regarded as friends of the slaves and abolitionists. As such they earned the distrust and dislike of the white colonists.

In some cases, the suspicion hardened into animosity and this was occasionally expressed in violence against the missionaries. The whites feared the influence of the missionaries whom they regarded as instigators and leaders of slave opposition. The missionaries thus earned the odium of slave-owners who considered them as enemies of the existing social order and a threat to the economic stability of the colonies.

Planters, however, sought to avoid open breaches of the laws of religious toleration (amongst Protestants) which were generally observed in the West Indies. They granted licences to the missionaries to perform their duties but the conditions imposed by these licences made them practically useless. For instance, missionaries were forbidden to preach unless they were specifically invited to do so by slave-owners or their attorneys. In addition, preaching after sunset was prohibited and baptisms could not be undertaken without the express permission of the slave master. In some colonies, such as in St. Vincent, penalties including fines, imprisonment, banishment and death (if the offender returned from banishment) were imposed on defaulting preachers.

The opposition of the planters and the restrictions imposed on the activities of the missionaries, made the results of their work, especially before 1800, less successful than it might otherwise have been. But the continued presence of missionaries in the several colonies was an indication of their interest in the religious welfare of the region.

Missionary activities were almost ignored by the elite class of whites, but among the slaves and among the free negroes and coloureds when they were given the opportunity, there was a consciousness of what they could achieve from learning. That the influence of the missionaries went further than the attendance at their chapels showed, became more and more evident as time passed.

After the abolition of the slave trade in 1808, missionary activities were increasingly encouraged by the slave-owners. Then it was no longer possible to replace legally through further purchase those slaves who had died, had run away, or had committed suicide, as a result of ill-usage. Slaves had to be better treated and missionaries were tolerated and encouraged in order that they might assist in getting slaves to work to the full. Even so, instruction to slaves was to be limited to what would make them more amenable to discipline and at the same time prevent them from contemplating hopeful alternatives to plantation labour or domestic pursuits.

5. Difficulties of the clergy and missionaries in British Colonies

(a) For a long time there was no effective central controlling authority which could direct the activities of the clergy and missionaries. The Bishop of London, for instance, did not control the appointment to Anglican benefices in the West Indies; he could, if he wished, advise and suggest, but he could not direct. Moreover, the mission churches were each independent.

(b) Both the clergy and missionaries were underpaid and overworked. The clergy, for example, until they received fixed endowments from the colonial legislatures, were supported by fees obtained by officiating at baptisms, marriages and funerals. But as far as work was concerned, one clergyman was clearly inadequate to serve all of the scattered islands of the British Virgin Islands.

(*c*) The clergy and missionaries often competed with each other in the conversion of negroes and often opposed each other's activities. The clergy tended to claim extra privileges as members of the state church.

(*d*) The attitude of both clergy and missionaries was sometimes detrimental to their success since many regarded their work merely as a career and lacked a sense of vocation.

(*e*) The religious apathy which was prevalent among the whites considerably reduced the effectiveness of the work of the clergy and missionaries.

(*f*) Indifference apart, the priests often met with the suspicion and hostility of the planters who looked upon their activities as a threat to the preservation of the social system and the institution of slavery. Slave revolts were often wrongly attributed to missionary influence. Restrictions were accordingly placed on their movements, and attendance of slaves at religious meetings depended on the slave-owners' consent. These requirements when enforced limited the growth of the missions.

(*g*) If the work of the church and chapel suffered from white intolerance, its progress was retarded by their lack of sound financial reserves.

(*h*) Unlike the clergy, the missionaries were not men of fixed status in the close-knit white society and were thus liable to obtain less sympathy from that society.

(*i*) The German Moravian missionaries suffered from the added disadvantage of being foreigners in the islands where they ministered, and their absorption was made far more difficult from the fact that unlike other white men, they engaged in manual work usually left to slaves and free negroes and coloureds.

(*j*) Quakers fought a losing battle in the British Virgin Islands because of the unique circumstances there: the islands were not particularly noted for their high moral virtues, and the temptations of illicit trading and the allurements of accumulated wealth were incompatible with the tenets of Quakerism.

(*k*) Many of the negroes did not remain converted but lapsed from membership and had to be excluded.

(*l*) Disciplinary exclusion apart, the growth of the chapel and church was also retarded by the transfer of members, usually slaves, from one island to another, and by death from epidemic diseases.

(*m*) The work of conversion and instruction was hampered by the negroes' ignorance of the preachers' languages and by the preachers' ignorance of the negroes' languages.

(*n*) West Indian society was marked by degeneracy and immorality, and preachers were faced with the difficult task of having to preserve their sense of dedication to religion and their moral righteousness. In seeking to do this by dissociating themselves from the main body of colonial whites, they denied themselves necessary support.

(*o*) Sickness, deprivation and death from tropical conditions and diseases were regular features in the lives of both clergy and missionaries.

Conclusions

The Catholic Church operated without competition in the Spanish American Empire, where it performed both religious and political functions. In religion, it taught and converted the native Indians to Christianity and catered to the religious needs of the Spanish community. Politically, it helped to extend the boundaries of Empire by removing opposition to it: in the case of the Indians by its teachings; and in the case of Europeans, largely through the operation of the Inquisition. In secular affairs, the Church built hospitals and almshouses, conducted schools of agriculture and industry, operated ranches and plantations and performed the functions of bankers. The Church did much good, but its efforts resulted in a number of drawbacks. For example, the genuineness of the conversion of Indians is doubtful, and the acquisition of the best land by the Church retarded the economic development of the colonies.

The British West Indian colonies were served by the Anglican Church and various missionary groups. The Anglican clergy catered more specifically to the needs of the white colonists. The missionaries directed their attention to the negro slaves. The work of the missionaries was largely that of preaching and conversion, but their efforts enabled the negroes to acquire training in leadership, and led them to discard their African practices to a large extent. The missionaries also built schools for the education of negroes.

The Anglican Church occupied a privileged place in the British colonies. In the colonies as in England it was the establishment church. For a long time the other nonconformist denominations had to suffer the opposition of the white colonists to their missionary activities, until eventually the slave-owners realised the usefulness of even non-conformist religions as a tool for making their slaves better workers.

In general therefore, in all the colonies, Spanish and British, the churches catered to spiritual needs at the same time as they contributed to the preservation of the society in which they operated.

Revision Questions

1. Compare the functions of the clergy in the Spanish and British colonies.
2. Compare the difficulties experienced by the church in Spanish America with those in the British West Indies.
3. In what ways did the Roman Catholic Church retard and promote the progress of the Spanish colonies?
4. The attitude of slave-owners to missionary efforts was generally favourable. How much truth is there in this statement?
5. Can it be said that missionaries served a useful purpose in the British West Indies?
6. What similar problems faced the clergy and missionaries in the West Indies?

7. The Mercantile System

The developing prosperity of the West Indian colonies not only influenced changes in the system of government but also the introduction of laws to secure the increasing profits of colonial trade to the governments of the colonising nations. Where the British and French were concerned, the enactment of legislation to regulate colonial trade followed the introduction of large-scale sugar-cane cultivation for export purposes from around the middle of the 17th century.

The essence of the mercantile system was that colonies were to be the economic complements of the imperial European nations. This meant, for instance, that colonies and mother-country would provide each other with the goods which each could not produce. Thus the colonies would provide tropical commodities in the form of foodstuffs and raw material, and the mother-country would provide manufactures and foodstuffs produced in temperate Europe. In this way each would satisfy the requirements of the other.

The mercantile system had a further important characteristic. It was generally considered that colonies were founded for the benefit of the respective mother-country. Colonial trade was therefore to be closely linked with that of the mother-country. This link was secured through appropriate legislation by all colonising European nations. But colonies were essentially subordinate to the mother-country and their subordination was expressed in restrictive trade regulations. Thus while the mother-country could engage in trade with any other nation, the colonies could not, on their own account, establish trade relations with whatever foreign country or colony they saw fit. Colonies were compelled to buy from and to sell to their respective mother-country. If foreign goods were desired, these could be obtained only through the mother-country. Direct trade with foreigners was illegal unless specially authorised by laws or other appropriate instructions.

The trade restrictions were expected to be of benefit to both the mother-country and the colonies. The former was able to secure both raw materials and a market free of competition for its manufactured goods. In return the latter were assured of defence against external enemy attack and a guaranteed market for their products.

The mercantile system, however, remained satisfactory to both colonists and European governments so long as it proved beneficial. Restrictions against foreign trade proved irksome to colonists especially in times of war or of depression in the market of the imperial power and when better opportunities for trade existed elsewhere. And unfavourable marketing opportunities contributed to the economic decline of the West Indies in the 19th century. The decline of the West Indies, in turn, meant a loss of trading benefits to the imperial powers since they obtained fewer tropical products and a smaller market for their manufactured goods. When this happened, European governments tended to reject their colonial responsibilities.

1. The Spanish system of trade

The economic policy of Spain with regard to the colonies accorded with current mercantilist ideas.

Colonies were esteemed chiefly because they were potential and actual sources of wealth and security to Spain. They offered closed markets to Spanish manufactures and agriculture and supplied such essential and luxury goods as cotton, dyes, hides, sugar, cocoa and tobacco. The colonies produced immense quantities of precious metals. Accordingly, a rigid and elaborate commercial system was established in order to create for Spain a monopoly of all trade and shipping with the colonies.

All trade from the colonies was reserved to the mother-country. Spain furnished the colonies with all the goods they required from Europe and these were shipped in Spanish vessels. The colonies produced in general only raw materials and articles that did not compete with the products of Spain. The export of gold and silver to foreign countries was forbidden. This policy of colonial monopoly lasted to the end of the colonial period.

The chief administrative agency for the regulation and development of commerce was the Casa de Contratacion or House of Trade established by royal decree on the 20th January, 1503. The Casa emerged as a government bureau empowered to license and supervise all ships, merchants, passengers, goods, crews and equipment passing between

Spain and the colonies. It enforced the laws and ordinances relating to commerce.

In Spain, as in other European countries, it was held that colonial commerce was the exclusive privilege of the mother-country. As such, foreign merchants were debarred or required a special royal licence before they could engage in Spanish colonial commerce.

Trade with the Spanish colonies was even more closely controlled. Traffic with America became to all intents and purposes a monopoly in the hands of the merchants of Seville and, later, of Cadiz. It was also made difficult or inconvenient for the small merchants to share directly in it by the requirement that only goods to a certain minimum value should be shipped to the colonies.

The policy of limiting transatlantic commerce to the cities of Seville and Cadiz was reflected in a similar policy in America. There trade was confined to three main centres, namely, Vera Cruz in New Spain, Cartagena in New Granada and Nombre de Dios on the Isthmus of Panama. This arrangement was undoubtedly adopted to secure greater ease in enforcing regulations, in preserving the Spanish monopoly and in preventing contraband trade. Caribbean seaports and the principal West Indian colonies were served by ships operating under special licence.

In an effort to enforce this limited-port policy and to protect vessels from pirates and privateers especially during wartime, a convoy system was developed. Though instituted in 1526, it was not until 1550 that the system was properly organised. The system remained officially in force for almost two hundred years. Special licences were granted occasionally to individual vessels sailing to minor ports.

In spite of the minute regulations and methods of supervision adopted, evasion was everywhere prevalent. This happened with or without the connivance of the royal officials. Large numbers of unlicensed persons engaged in contraband trade with the colonies. Their activities received encouragement from the colonists who disliked trade restrictions.

The exclusive trade policy led to difficulties. With the decline of Spanish industries which made it difficult for Spain to supply its own much less colonial needs, the colonists had recourse to foreign sources. A widespread contraband trade developed. Illicit traffic was carried on by the English, French and Dutch. It was generally welcomed by the colonists who thereby obtained a wider variety of goods at more reasonable prices than those obtained through legitimate channels.

The exclusive trade policy also led to deficiencies both of goods and of capital. Smuggling could not always satisfy the needs of the colonists who were kept more or less understocked and had to pay exorbitant prices for all European commodities. These conditions were the most serious obstacles to the growth of industry, population and well-being in the colonies.

Whatever may have been the aims of the commercial system when first formulated, it proved inadequate to maintain or promote the prosperity of Spain or of its colonies. This was because its rigidity led to its continuous evasion.

2. Reasons for the British Navigation Acts of the 1650's and 1660's

Two fundamental factors governed the introduction of the British Navigation Acts of the 1650's and 1660's. These were, firstly, the need to exclude Dutch (and by implication other foreign) competition from the trade of the British West Indies, and secondly, the need to draw closer the bonds of empire in order to bring the colonies more directly under central control exercised from London.

By the middle of the 17th century, the Dutch dominated West Indian trade just as they dominated the fisheries of northern Europe, the trade with the spice islands of the Far East and the slave trade with Africa. The Dutch were able to achieve this position of ascendancy by virtue of their powerful and efficient mercantile navy, the establishment of strategic trading entrepots on the islands of Curacao, Saba, St. Martin and St. Eustatius, and their ability to trade on more favourable terms than other mercantile and colonial European nations. Owing to lower freight rates, more abundant capital and a more efficient system of credit, the Dutch monopolised to a marked degree the West Indian carrying trade. For their own commercial advantage the Dutch promoted British settlements and cultivation by providing equipment and supplies and restored planters' finances with credit when necessary. They also introduced sugar-cane into the West Indies in the early 1640's, and sugar increased the commercial importance of the West Indian colonies.

By 1650, the commercial supremacy of the Dutch was a formidable obstacle to England's economic development and to its creation of a powerful self-sufficient commercial empire. By then, a considerable portion of England's trade was being carried in Dutch ships. During the Civil Wars in England in the 1640's, colonial commercial regulations had been disregarded and Dutch merchants had secured a large share of the trade with British West Indian colonies. It was necessary after the end of the Civil Wars to recapture this trade, considerably heightened in importance as it was since the introduction of sugar about a decade before.

The second factor was closely related to the first. Under prevailing economic theory, colonies existed for the benefit of the mother-country. The colonies were to produce the goods which England could not produce and England was to control the carrying trade. In addition, the most valuable colonial products were offered a guaranteed market in England. In turn, England insisted on a corresponding market monopoly in the British West Indies for its manufactured goods. The system was one of Empire preference. In order to exclude the Dutch and other possible foreign competitors from the British colonial trade, the British Government sought by means of the Navigation Laws to bind the economies of the West Indian and other colonies to that of England in a unified Empire. By means of specialisation of the various parts, the different colonies providing different raw materials and Britain supplying manufactured goods, the Empire would be better able to withstand foreign competition in peace-time and enemy attack during war.

The advantages envisaged from the exclusion of foreigners from the colonial trade were economic, political and military. Economically, an enlarged consumption by colonists of British manufactures would increase the business of merchants and traders, while increased trade generally would employ more British shipping and crews. Larger customs revenue would also be obtained from an augmented trade. Closer commercial relations would inevitably lead to closer political ties between the colonies and Britain. With the exclusion of continental European nations from the British West Indies, the trade of the colonies would become centralised in a few clearly defined trade routes radiating from Britain. Militarily, this would facilitate Britain's role of defending colonial trade against pirate and enemy attack.

3. The principal features of the British Mercantile System

By the middle of the 17th century, the West Indies were beginning to show their potential as plantation colonies. Their increasing wealth prompted the English Government to draw its colonies more and more under central control. This was especially necessary since the Dutch with their greater trading ability dominated the trade of the British West Indies. The regulation of trade was another aspect of Cromwellian imperialism which was shown in his policy of colonial conquest known as the 'Western Design' and which found culmination in the capture of Jamaica in 1655. Cromwell's system of trade regulations was continued by Charles II.

The principal features of the British Mercantile System were embodied in the Navigation Acts of 1651, 1660, 1663, and 1673, but in their spirit and definition these Acts owe their origin to others passed earlier in the 17th century. These earlier acts had been formulated with regard to tobacco and were at first applied to the American mainland colonies. They were later applied to the British West Indies. In 1621, regulations confined exported colonial tobacco exclusively to England. In 1624 and 1625 further regulations forbade the importation of foreign tobacco into England. These later regulations were subsequently relaxed, but foreign tobacco became subject to discriminatory duties. Despite attempts to enforce these regulations they were widely evaded. The methods of enforcement included the exaction of bonds and the establishment of naval patrols.

The Navigation Act of 1651 prohibited the importation of colonial products into England except in English ships. Further, it confined the export of European goods to British colonies to English ships or ships of the country where the goods originated.

The Navigation Act of 1660 extended and added to the provisions of the 1651 Act. Henceforth, no goods could be imported into or exported from any British colony except in vessels of British, Irish or colonial origin. The master and three-fourths of the crew of such vessels had to be British. Furthermore, aliens were prohibited from acting as factors or merchants in the colonies. In addition, the Act provided that certain enumerated articles—sugar, cottonwool, tobacco, indigo, ginger, fustic and other dye-woods—could be shipped only to England, Ireland or to any other English colony. To prevent smuggling, captains engaged in British West Indian trade were required to give bonds worth £1,000 or £2,000 which were forfeited if the law was broken.

Despite the restrictions of the Act of 1660, direct trade between Europe and the British West Indies continued. To curb this illegal trade, the Staple Act of 1663 was passed. This Act specified that all goods, both British and non-British, which were intended for the colonies had to be shipped from a British port. Direct trade between Europe and the colonies was forbidden. The only exceptions were goods whose importation for consumption in England was forbidden.

The Act of Navigation (1660) caused certain definite inconveniences for which a remedy was necessary. For instance, restricted goods could be illegally sold to foreigners under cover of inter-colonial trade. That is, colonial goods ostensibly consigned to another British colony, could be carried to foreign ports and there sold more cheaply than goods paying customs duties. To end this traffic the British Parliament passed the Plantations Duties Act of 1673, imposing a substantial export duty on all the commodities enumerated in the Act of 1660, and including coconuts also, when shipped from one colony to another.

These Acts formed the basis of the British Mercantile System and remained virtually intact until they were repealed in 1849. Later in the 17th century, a special official—the Clerk to the Naval Office—was appointed in each colony to supervise the operation of the Acts, and in 1693, Courts of Vice-Admiralty were provided to punish breaches of the Acts.

In return for the restrictions on their commerce which the Acts imposed, the colonies were guaranteed a market for their products in England, and protection against enemy attack by the British navy.

4. Effects of the Navigation Laws upon British West Indian planters and merchants

The Navigation Laws passed after 1650 started an economic and trade war against the Dutch who had hitherto dominated British West Indian trade. The laws were reinforced by a number of naval wars in which Dutch maritime and trade supremacy were dealt crippling blows. Dutch traders were dismissed from the English islands and Dutch shipping excluded. Colonial trade was confined by law to British shipping. The net result of the policy of exclusion was that the advantages hitherto enjoyed by planters through contact with the Dutch in the form of lower freight rates, more abundant capital, and a more efficient system of credit, were removed.

Under the Navigation Laws, the British colonies were tied in close relationship to Britain. But the contact was not one of equality. The economic interests of the colonies were subordinated to those of the mother-country. Whenever there was a conflict of interest between colony and mother-country, the former was necessarily subordinated to the latter. As compensation for restrictions on the trade of the colonies, England provided them with the necessary means of defence and guaranteed them a protected market for the main colonial commodities. Defence of the islands was important since by safeguarding the islands England enabled the means of existence of the planters to continue.

England was not unique in passing restrictions or monopolistic trade regulations. Such regulations were in accordance with prevailing economic theories of colonisation; and other European nations which had colonies, such as Spain and France, imposed similar regulations. And any disruption of the channels of trade would adversely affect the islands, dependent as they were on trade for their welfare.

Because of the restrictions imposed on trade and in particular on the staple products of the several colonies, it was evident that the condition of the British market would naturally determine the prospect of profitable cultivation in the colonies. It would mean, for instance, that if prices and demand were high, a stimulus would be given to plantation agriculture, and that, alternatively, if prices and demand were low, the disincentive could lead to economic depression in the West Indies. After the 1660's West Indian agriculture was considerably influenced by this factor.

From the middle of the 17th century, sugar came to dominate British West Indian economy. The British market for this commodity, though growing, did not keep pace with the colonist's rapidly increasing output and prices fell as supply outgrew demand. From the 1660's to the late 1680's, prices tended to decline slowly, but not to the extent of discouraging production. Output increased steadily and by the beginning of the 18th century, British trade with the West Indian colonies exceeded in quantity and value the trade with the North American colonies.

The 18th century European wars (in which the West Indies were affected as colonies of participating nations) proved of mixed blessing to the British West Indian planters when taken in conjunction with the trade laws. The curtailment of supplies from the non-British West Indian islands when these were captured by Britain was a benefit. The subsequent shortage of supplies in Europe enabled a greater quantity of British West Indian products to reach continental markets via Britain. This not only led to higher prices and consequently greater profits to British West Indian planters, but also stimulated the expansion of cultivation.

However, under the Navigation Laws, the islands were restricted to buying European manufactures from or through Britain only. These supplies were sometimes disrupted during war-time, when British vessels were attacked by enemy warships and privateers.

Two further ways in which the Navigation Acts proved disastrous to the British West Indies can be illustrated by reference to the consequences of the American War of Independence and of the French Revolutionary and Napoleonic Wars.

Under the Navigation Acts, trade was permitted between one British colony and another. Under these regulations a profitable trade had developed between the British American colonies and the British West Indies, sugar and molasses from the latter being exchanged for essential foodstuffs and plantation supplies from the former. The Declaration of Independence by the American colonies in 1776 and its confirmation in 1783, placed the United States beyond the pale of the Navigation Acts. The trade between the United States and the British West Indies was consequently severed, resulting in considerable suffering to the planters and their slaves.

British West Indian planters were not permitted to bargain on their own account. Under the Navigation Laws direct trade between the British West Indies and Europe was forbidden. West Indian produce, therefore, had to find its way to Europe via Britain. Planters' profits were thus limited to the extent that Britain sought and found the best market. The outbreak of war between Britain and France in 1793 was at first favourable to the British West Indies since a very profitable market was found for their commodities in Europe when Britain captured the French colonies. But awareness of the increasing profitability of the European market, especially in sugar, led to the development of other areas of cultivation in the East and West Indies and to the promotion of beet-sugar production in Europe. These developments were to lead to depression in British West Indian plantation agriculture and to the eventual economic decline of the islands.

The fortunes of the merchants tended to follow the same course as those of the planters. This was because of the close relationship which existed between the two groups. From the very beginning of English settlement, merchants financed the estates. Sometimes they lent money to prospective planters at high rates of interest. Sometimes they went into partnership, one partner going out to manage the plantation while the other remained behind in England to sell the produce and to ship plantation supplies. In these instances, the fortune of one depended upon the fortune of the other. If each shared in the actual profits of the plantation, he also shared in the losses. Inasmuch as the Navigation Laws contributed to the prosperity or decline of West Indian planters, they contributed to a similar fate of the merchants.

Conclusion

The essence of the mercantile system was the preservation of colonial trade, both import and export, for the benefit of the imperial power. As such, foreigners were not to be allowed to compete. In the case of the English colonies, the most formidable competitors were the Dutch, and Dutch commercial supremacy prevented England from deriving full benefit from its colonies. Control of colonial trade could also enable Britain to exercise greater political control over its colonies and give employment to more Englishmen and English ships. Consequently, in the 1650's and 1660's a number of Navigation Acts were passed confining colonial trade in specified colonial products to Britain, and forbidding trade with foreigners. By so doing, the Acts were supposed to guarantee to the colonies a ready market for their produce, but the trade restrictions naturally caused hardship and loss when this trade was disrupted by war and when more favourable markets could be obtained elsewhere than in Britain.

The Spanish system of trade was even more restrictive than that of Britain, for not only was it confined to Spain, but it was further restricted to certain Spanish ports only. Moreover, trade was under the exclusive control of a single institution, the Casa de Contratacion. The basic reason was that Spain wanted to preserve its trading monopoly in the West Indies and to exclude other European nations. It was unable to do so, however, and so it introduced the convoy system to protect its trading vessels and minimise loss. Despite the trade regulations, the inability of Spain to satisfy colonial needs led to the development of a contraband trade between Spanish colonists and foreign Europeans. This illicit trade, in turn, retarded the growth of industry and population in the Spanish colonies.

Revision Questions

1. Why did European nations seek to control trade for their own benefit?
2. Account for Dutch trading supremacy in the West Indies in the 17th century.
3. What methods were adopted by European nations to protect their trade? Name the dangers against which it was necessary to provide safeguards?
4. What differences existed between British and Spanish trade regulations?
5. How important was the West Indian trade with North America in the 18th century?
6. How was trade affected by the wars of the 18th century?

List of
Short Note Topics

The following topics have been taken from past examination papers. They are included here to encourage students to find out facts for themselves and as a revision aid for examinations. They should be useful to both teachers and students.

Some of the subjects listed below are not covered in this book and will require outside reading. Students should write brief notes on each topic. These notes will serve as useful revision material and examination preparation.

1. Discovery and Rivalry

1. Pope Alexander VI
2. Bulls of demarcation
3. Treaty of Tordesillas
4. La Navidad
5. Don Nicolas de Ovando
6. Gonzalo de Oviedo
7. Balboa
8. Cabral Pedro Menendez de Aviles
9. Francois le Clerc
10. Guarda-costas
11. Drake at Cartagena
12. The legend of El Dorado
13. Raleigh in the West Indies
14. Bahama Passage
15. Piet Heyn
16. Sir Thomas Warner
17. Sir William Courteen
18. The Earl of Carlisle
19. Captain John Powell
20. D'Esnambuc
21. Barbadian Royalists and the Declaration of Independence, 1651
22. Capture of Jamaica by the English
23. Admiral Penn and General Venables
24. Port Royal and Tortuga
25. Flibustiers
26. Sir Henry Morgan and Panama

27. Admiral Benbow
28. British gains in the Treaty of Utrecht
29. The Battle of Saints
30. Nelson's dockyard
31. Admiral Vernon and Cartagena
32. St. Lucia, 1783–1815
33. Neutral islands
34. British Navy in the Caribbean
35. Militias

2. The Plantation System

1. Arawaks and Caribs
2. Encomienda system
3. Indentured labour
4. Richard Ligon
5. Teaché
6. Curing house
7. Wind mills
8. Labour-saving devices
9. Molasses and rum
10. Bryan Edwards
11. Cuban sugar
12. Sugar-beet
13. The West Indian Lobby
14. Effects of hurricanes
15. Bill of exchange
16. Absentee landlordism
17. Book-keepers
18. Ratoons

3. Slavery

1. Slave forts and factories
2. National Trading Companies
3. The Royal African Company
4. Ashantis
5. Barracoon
6. Slave coffle
7. Whydah
8. Middle Passage
9. Asiento
10. 'Seasoning'
11. 'Code Noir'
12. 'Refuse' fish
13. Ackee and breadfruit
14. Dutch stripes and Guinée Bleue
15. Deficiency Laws
16. Sunday market
17. Obeahman
18. Free blacks and free coloureds
19. Grand blancs and petit blancs
20. 'Great house'
21. Barrack housing
22. The Jamaican Maroons
23. Cudjoe
24. Bush negroes
25. Black Caribs
26. Amis des Noirs
27. Oge and the mulattoes of St. Domingue
28. The Dominican Revolt
29. Toussaint L'Ouverture
30. Henri Christophe
31. The Society for Effecting the Abolition of the Slave Trade
32. George Fox
33. Clapham Sect
34. The Case of James Somerset
35. Thomas Clarkson
36. The Mansfield Judgement
37. The Abolition Act, 1807
38. The Kitty's Amelia
39. Christmas Rebellion in Jamaica
40. Mico Trust
41. Emancipation Act, 1833

4. Apprenticeship

1. Lord Stanley
2. James Stephen (Jr.)
3. Apprentices
4. Ancillary Acts of Emancipation
5. Slave compensation commissioners
6. 'Architects of freedom'
7. Negro Education Grant
8. Full emancipation

5. Colonial Government

1. Vice-roys and Captains-General
2. Council of the Indies
3. Audiencias
4. Cabildos
5. Lords-Proprietors
6. Campbell of Grenada
7. House of Assembly
8. Board of Council
9. Colonel Parke of the Leeward Islands
10. A Colonial Act
11. Board of Trade and Plantation
12. Secretary of State for the Colonies
13. Crown Colony
14. Legislative Council
15. Governor's Commission and Instructions

6. Religious Denominations

1. Las Casas
2. Montesinos
3. The Spanish Inquisition
4. The Moravians
5. The Wesleyan Methodists
6. The Quakers
7. The Anglicans
8. The Roman Catholics
9. William Knibb
10. Rev. James Ramsay
11. George Lisle and Moses Baker
12. Rev. John Smith
13. Colonial Church Union
14. Church and Chapel
15. Baptism of slaves
16. The denominations and education
17. Missionary societies

7. The Mercantile System

1. Casa de Contratacion
2. Convoys
3. Providence Island Company
4. Punta del Araya
5. Dutch West India Company
6. Isles of America Company
7. Colbert's policies towards the West Indies
8. Navigation Laws
9. Enumerated commodities
10. Clerk to the Naval Office
11. Molasses Act, 1733
12. British Free Port Act, 1766
13. The Free Port System
14. Packets
15. Vice-Admiralty Courts
16. The Sugar Act, 1764
17. Factors
18. Dutch entrepots
19. Mercantilism

A Select Bibliography

This list is by no means exhaustive. It consists of only the primary and most important sources used in the preparation of this text. The three general works on West Indian history are given first. Thereafter the more specialised studies are given in alphabetical order by authors.

General Works:

1. F. R. Augier, S. C. Gordon, D. G. Hall, and M. Reckord, *The Making of the West Indies* (Longmans, London, 1960).

2. J. H. Parry and P. M. Sherlock, *A Short History of the West Indies* (Macmillan, London, 1957).

3. D. A. G. Waddell, *The West Indies & The Guianas* (Prentice Hall, Englewood Cliffs, New Jersey, 1967).

Special Studies:

1. Morley Ayearst, *The British West Indies: The Search for Self Government* (Allen & Unwin, London, 1960).

2. Philip D. Curtin, *Two Jamaicas. The Role of Ideas in a Tropical Colony, 1830–1865* (Harvard University Press, Cambridge, Mass. 1955).

3. Elsa V. Goveia, *Slave Society in the British Leeward Islands at the end of the Eighteenth Century* (Yale University Press, New Haven, 1965).

4. Douglas Hall, *Free Jamaica 1830–1865: An Economic History* (Yale University Press, New Haven, 1959).

5. C. H. Haring, *The Spanish Empire in America* (New York, 1947).

6. C. H. Haring, *The Buccaneers in the West Indies in the XVIIth Century* (Archon Books, Hamden, Connecticut, 1966).

7. Gordon K. Lewis, *The Growth of the Modern West Indies* (MacGibbon & Kee, London, 1968).

8. L. G. Leyburn: *The Haitian People* (Yale University Press, New Haven, 1948).

9. A. P. Newton, *The European Nations in the West Indies* (London, 1933; Black, London, 1966).

10. Lowell J. Ragatz, *The Fall of the Planter Class in the British Caribbean, 1763–1833* (Washington, D.C., 1928; reprinted New York, 1963).

11. F. G. Spurdle, *Early West Indian Government, Showing the Progress of Government in Barbados, Jamaica and the Leeward Islands, 1660–1783* (New Zealand; not dated).

12. Eric Williams, *Capitalism and Slavery* (University of North Carolina Press, Chapel Hill, 1944; Deutsch, London, 1964).

Examination Questions

The following questions have been selected from past General Certificate of Education examination papers. Though an attempt has been made to classify them according to subject matter, it should be noted that in some instances, questions refer to several topics. Answers should make allowance for this.

1 Discovery and Rivalry

1. What geographical ideas influenced Columbus and what discoveries did he make on his four voyages? (Cambridge, June, 1970)

2. What did Columbus discover and what did he achieve as a result of each of his four voyages to the Caribbean? (London, Summer, 1968)

3. How did other European nations react to the growth of the Spanish power and what actions did they take to weaken it? (London, January, 1968)

4. Give an account of the activities of French and English privateers in the Caribbean from 1500 to 1600. What did they achieve by their activities? (London, January, 1969)

5. Describe the illegal trade and privateering carried on in the Caribbean by the enemies of Spain in the second half of the 16th century. (Cambridge, June, 1969)

6. Outline the aims and achievements of the French and the Dutch in the Caribbean to the middle of the 17th century. (London, January, 1970)

7. What did pirates and buccaneers seek to achieve in the 16th and 17th centuries? How far did they succeed? (London, Summer, 1969)

8. Who were the buccaneers, and how did they help the interests of England and France in the Caribbean? (Cambridge, June, 1969)

9. What were the chief contributions of the Dutch to Caribbean history before 1650? (London, January, 1969)

10. What part did the Caribbean colonies play in the Seven Years' War (1756–1763) and in the War of American Independence (1775–1783)? (London, Summer, 1968)

11. How were the British West Indian islands affected by the War of American Independence? (Cambridge, June, 1969)

12. Show the effects upon the West Indies of (*a*) the achievement of independence by the Thirteen Colonies, and (*b*) the wars with the French Republic and Napoleon. (London, Summer, 1969)

13. How were the Caribbean islands defended by land and sea in the wars of the 18th century? (Cambridge, June, 1970)

14. What changes in ownership of West Indian territories took place after *two* of the following wars:

(i) The Seven Years' War (1756–1763);
(ii) The War of American Independence (1775–1783);
(iii) The Revolutionary and Napoleonic Wars (1793–1815)?

Explain the importance of the changes you describe. (Cambridge, June, 1970)

2 The Plantation System

1. What were the principal exports of the Spanish from the Caribbean in the 16th century? (London, Summer, 1966)

2. Why did early English and French settlers make their homes in the West Indies, and what were some of the difficulties they had to meet? (London, January, 1968)

3. Compare and contrast the *early* problems of settlement experienced by the English in St. Kitts and Barbados. (Cambridge, June, 1970)

4. What part did the Dutch play in the change from tobacco planting to sugar planting in the West Indies? Why was the change made and what were its effects upon the white population of the islands? (London, Summer, 1968)

5. What were the good effects and the bad effects of the establishment of sugar as the main crop in the West Indies? (London, January, 1970)

6. Give an account of the activities on a sugar plantation during crop time in the 18th century. (Cambridge, June, 1969)

7. For what reasons were plantation owners dissatisfied in the late 18th century? (London, January, 1969)

8. Were the British or the French colonies in the West Indies likely to be the more prosperous after 1763? Give reasons for your choice. (London, January, 1968)

9. Compose an advertisement for insertion in a local newspaper for the sale of a sugar plantation in the year 1815. (Cambridge, June, 1969)

10. What economic difficulties faced the British West Indies in the years 1783–1833? (London, January, 1970)

11. What difficulties did the planters in the British West Indian islands experience in the profitable production of sugar in the period 1800–1830? (Cambridge, June, 1970)

3 and 4 Slavery and the Apprenticeship System

1. What do you understand by the problem of labour supply before 1783? How was the problem met by the use of (*a*) the native Indians, (*b*) indentured servants, and (*c*) slaves? (London, Summer, 1969)

2. As a captain of a slaver write an account of a voyage from West Africa to the Caribbean in the 18th century. (Cambridge, June, 1970)

3. Describe the way in which life and work were organised in a large sugar plantation in the middle of the 18th century. (London, Summer, 1968)

4. Describe the provisions of the 'Code Noir' and compare these with laws enacted by the British islands to regulate the life of the slaves. (Cambridge, June, 1969)

5. How and why did the British Government (*a*) abolish the slave trade in 1807 and (*b*) emancipate the slaves in 1833 ? (London, January, 1969)

6. What suggestions were made before 1833 for the 'amelioration' of the slaves' hardships? Why did this policy not prevent the passing of the Act which abolished slavery? (London, Summer, 1968)

7. Show the connection of each of the following with the movement for the abolition of slavery: the Quakers; the Moravians; the Baptist Missionary Society; the Society for Effecting the Abolition of the Slave Trade. (London, Summer, 1969)

8. What were the duties of the Special (i.e. Stipendiary) Magistrates? How far were they successful? (London, Summer, 1968)

9. Explain the chief problems that arose over the apprenticeship scheme, and why this was ended in 1838. (Cambridge, June, 1969)

10. Putting yourself in the role of an English visitor to the area during August, 1838, write a newspaper article giving the reactions of an estate owner, a missionary, and a former field slave to the coming of 'full freedom.' (Cambridge, June, 1970)

5 Colonial Government

1. How did Spain organise the government of her American empire in the 16th and 17th centuries? (Cambridge, June, 1970)

2. Describe the system by which the Spanish governed their Caribbean empire and show how they regulated its trade and shipping. (London, January, 1969)

3. How did the European powers seek to control the government of their Caribbean colonies in the 17th century? (London, Summer, 1968)

4. Describe the extent and nature of the control exercised in the West Indies during the early 18th century by European governments. (London, January, 1970)

5. Give an account of the form of government in the (Caribbean) islands under British rule in the 18th century. (London, January, 1968)

6. Write a letter from the Governor of a British West Indian island in the year 1708 (to the Board of Trade in London) explaining the difficulties he has encountered in his dealings with the House of Assembly. (Cambridge, June, 1969)

7. Why were West Indians in the mid-19th century critical of (*a*) Crown Colony Government and (*b*) the assemblies in islands such as Jamaica? Make clear in your answer how these systems of government differed. (London, Summer, 1968)

8. What is meant by 'Crown Colony Government?' Why was it so widely established in the 19th century and what were its merits and defects? (London, Summer, 1969)

6 The Religious Denominations

1. Why, and how, did the Catholic Church try to protect the native peoples of the Spanish-American empire? (Cambridge, June, 1969)

2. What religious policies were adopted by the various European governments in the West Indies in the 17th century? (London, Summer, 1966)

3. What differences existed in the attitude of the planters to (*a*) the clergy of the Anglican and Catholic Churches and (*b*) the missionaries? (London, Summer, 1966)

4. Indicate the difficulties of missionaries at the end of the 18th century. (London, January, 1968)

5. What difficulties were experienced by the missionaries in their work among the slaves at the beginning of the 19th century? (Cambridge, June, 1969)

6. Describe the principal activities of missionaries in the West Indies between 1783 and 1833. (London, January, 1969)

7 The Mercantile System

1. How did the European powers seek to control the trade of their Caribbean colonies in the 17th century? (London, Summer, 1968)

2. Describe Britain's trading policy in the West Indies. (London, January, 1969)

3. How did European governments endeavour to keep the profits of their own colonies, and what effects did this policy have upon merchants and planters in the West Indies? (London, Summer, 1966)

4. Explain Mercantilism. What were the effects of this system upon (a) Caribbean colonies and (b) mother countries? (London, Summer, 1969)

5. Give an account of the trading relations between the Caribbean and the North American mainland in the 18th century. (London, Summer, 1968)

Index

Abolition of slave trade 57, 59, 62, 83–5
  terms of the Act (1807) 85
Absentee landlordism 56, 58, 77
amelioration in the British colonies 86–7
  in the French colonies 91
Anglican church 124, 125, 128, 130–1, 134
Anguilla 18
Antigua 20, 23, 32, 40, 120, 129
Anti-Slavery Society 87, 88, 99–100
apprenticeship, aims of 94–5

  end of 99–100
  meaning 93
Arawaks 22 *See also* Indians
Aruba 20, 27
Asia, land routes to 11
  products from 11
'asiento' 36, 37, 64, 66
audiencia 15, 106
Avila, Don Juan 26

Bahia 27
Barbados 20, 23, 32, 36, 40, 50, 77, 110, 120

barracoons 62, 66
Bathurst, Lord (Secretary of State for the Colonies) and amelioration 86
Battle of the Saints (1782) 39
Battle of Trafalgar (1805) 41
beet sugar 42, 48, 57, 101
Bermuda 39, 40
Berrio, Antonio de 20
Bogle, Paul 119, 120
Bonaire 20, 27
Boukman 80
Brazil 13, 25, 26, 27, 42, 65, 81
British Honduras 35
British Royal African Company 65–6
buccaneers 23–5, 50
Burke, Edmund 89

cabildo 108
Cadiz 138
Canaries 26
Cape Verde Islands 26
Caribs 22, 23, 37, 46 See also Indians
Cartagena 15, 17, 19, 28, 37, 138
Chinese (indentures) 101
Civil War (United States, 1861–5) 118–119
Clapham Sect 88
Clarkson, Thomas 84, 88
'Code Noir' 73–6
    disability clauses 74
    beneficent clauses 74–5, 79
Codrington Plantation 77
Colbert 30, 79, 121
Colonial administration, British 109–118
    French 120–2
    Spanish 105–9
colonial assembly 56, 70, 79, 80, 87, 105, 110, 113–14, 115, 120, 122, 128, 130
colonial council 56, 70, 105, 111–12, 120, 121–2, 128, 130
Colonial Office 104, 113–14
colonies, value of 44, 104, 111
Columbus, Christopher 13, 21, 104
Compagnie des Indes Occidentales 121
Company of the Isles of America 120–1
Company of St. Christopher 120
compensation for slaves 90
contraband trade 28, 29, 37, 138
convoy system 17, 29, 37, 138
Council of the Indies 15, 105, 109
Cowper, William 85
Cromwell, Oliver 20, 30, 31, 140

Crown Colony Government, advantages of 116
    disadvantages of 117–18
    introduction of 114–16, 120
Cuba 13, 14, 15, 19, 21, 26, 41, 42, 81
Curacao 18, 20, 27, 29, 32, 139

Deficiency Laws 50, 64, 77
Denmark 85
D'Esnambuc 20, 120
Dessalines 81
'directeurs' 104
Dolben, Sir William 84
Dominica 21, 23, 35, 37, 38, 39, 40
Drake, Sir Francis 17–18, 28
Dutch, and the British Navigation Laws 139, 140, 142
    and the slave trade 65
    promotion of settlement and trade 26–8
    promotion of sugar production 49, 51
    naval activities 25–6, 27
    role in the West Indies 25–8
Dutch Wars 21, 24, 30–4
Dutch West India Company 24, 27, 34, 49

Earl of Carlisle 109
emancipation, in the British colonies 59, 62, 92, 93
    British Act of Emancipation 89–90
    factors influencing 87–9
    in Jamaica 118
    in the French colonies 90–1, 92
Eyre, Governor E. J. 119, 120
England 14
    reaction to Spanish monopoly 17–18, 20

factors 58, 66
Fajardo 26
Ferdinand, King of Spain 13
'flotas' 37
Fox, Charles James 85, 89
France, reaction to Spanish monopoly 17–18, 20
free-coloureds 62, 69
    disabilities of 70, 79–80, 112, 122
free negroes 62, 69
    disabilities of 70, 112, 122, 129
free ports 42, 55
French Revolution (1789) 80, 84, 90
full freedom, introduction of 99–100
    its aftermath 100–2

Gordon, George William 119, 120

Gordon, William (Stipendiary Magistrate, British Virgin Islands) 98

Gouvenot, Laurent de 64

governor (colonial) 36, 51, 106–8, 110, 111, 114, 116, 117, 120–1

Greater Antilles 19, 21, 25

Grenada 21, 38, 39, 40, 120

Grenadines 38, 39, 40

Guadeloupe 18, 20, 23, 38, 41, 58, 120, 121, 122

Guiana colonies (Essequibo, Demerara, Berbice) 39, 41, 85, 86, 101, 115, 120

'guarda costas' 15, 28, 35

Haiti *see* St. Domingue

Havana 15, 28, 36, 37, 38, 39

Hawkins, Sir John 17, 28

Heemskerck, Admiral Jacob van 26

Heyn, Piet 27

Hispaniola 13, 14, 15, 19, 21, 24, 26, 32

Holmes, Captain Robert 31

House of Trade (Casa de Contratacion) 15, 106, 137

humanitarians 62, 88, 93, 100

Indians, as labourers 63, 64, 83, 106, 126, 127

    impact of Europeans on 14

indentured labourers 61, 63–4, 83, 101, 119

Industrial Revolution 34, 47, 92

Inquisition 15, 126

Isabella, Queen of Spain 13

Ita, Peter 27

Jamaica 13, 14, 20, 21, 24, 25, 29, 32, 36, 40, 42, 77, 81, 97, 99, 101, 111, 118, 120, 140

Ketelhodt, Baron von 119, 120

Knibb, William 88

Labour problems after emancipation 100

labour-saving devices 52, 57–8, 72

laissez-faire 59, 62, 89, 92, 95

Las Casas 63, 83

Le Clerc, Francois 17

Le Clerc, General 81

Leeward Islands 32, 36, 48, 77, 128–9

Lesser Antilles, settlement of 18, 19–20

    Spanish neglect of 21–2

Letter of marque 17

letter-patent 112–13

line of demarcation 13

Loncq, Hendrick 27

Lord-Proprietor 50, 104, 109–10, 111

L'Ouverture, Toussaint 81

Mansfield, Lord (Chief Justice) 84, 88

Maroons 77, 81

Martinique 18, 20, 23, 33, 38, 41, 58, 91, 120, 121, 122

marcantile system 136–7

'metairie' system 101

Methodist 128, 131–2

'Middle Passage' 61, 68, 82

missionaries 44, 86, 128, 131–4

    and the abolition of the slave trade 129, 132

    attitude of planters to 72, 128, 131–2

    difficulties of 132–4

    position in society 69–70

Money Bill 112, 114

Montesinos 63

Montserrat 18, 20, 32, 33, 39, 40

Morant Bay Uprising 118–20

Moravians 128, 129, 131–2, 133

Mosquito Coast 24, 37

Navigation Acts 30, 51, 55, 113

    effects on merchants and planters 142–4

    provisions of Acts 141, 142, 144

    reasons for passing 139–140

Nevis 20, 32, 33, 39, 40

Netherlands 14

    reaction to Spanish monopoly 16–18, 20, 25

    See also, Dutch and Dutch West India Company

Nombre de Dios 138

Ogé 80

old representative System 51, 111–13, 116

Order in Council 85, 86

Panama 18, 28

papal bulls 9, 13, 14–15, 16, 61, 64

Penn, Admiral 20

pirates 17, 18

Pitt, William 85, 89

plantation 44

    layout and organisation 51–3

Plantations Duties Act (1673) 141
Pope Alexander VI 13, 26, 64
Port Royal 24
Portugal, and the slave trade 61, 64, 65
    influence on Columbus' voyages
        10
    rivalry and international dispute
        with Spain 13
    smuggling 17, 25
Portuguese indentures 101
Powell, Captain John 20
Puerto Bello 28, 37
privateers 17, 18, 37, 38, 39, 40
proprietary government 51, 109–10,
    121
provincial governor (Spanish) 106–7
Puerto Rico 13, 14, 15, 19, 21, 27, 28,
    41, 81
Punta del Araya 26

Quakers, and slavery 84, 88, 133

Ramsay, James 84, 88
Reformation 16
religious instruction, 72, 86, 124–5, 126,
    127, 128–9
Renaissance (Rebirth of Learning) 11
revolts, by slaves 79
Rodney, Admiral George 39
Roman Catholic Church 15, 124
    role in Spanish American Empire
        125–7, 130, 134
runaways 75, 78, 80
Ruyter, Admiral de 32, 33

Saba 20, 32, 139
St. Bartholomew 38
St. Christopher (St. Kitts) 18, 20, 22–3,
    27, 32, 36, 39, 40
St. Domingue 24, 38
    economy destroyed 81, 91
    political independence of 81
    revolt in (1791) 41, 62, 77, 79–81
St. Eustatius 18, 20, 32, 39, 139
St. Lucia 21, 23, 35, 37, 38, 39, 40, 41,
    86, 115
St. Martin 18, 20, 27, 139
St. Vincent 21, 23, 35, 37, 38, 39, 40,
    132
San Juan del Puerto Rico 15, 18, 19
San Juan de Ulua 28
Santiago de Cuba 15, 37
Santo Domingo 15, 17, 19, 28
Seville 138

Sharp, Granville 84, 88
Sierra Leone, negro settlement in 88
Siete Partidas 73
slave factories 66
slave forts 62, 66
slaves 50, 51, 61, 63
    clothing 62, 71, 82, 83, 90
    education 72, 82, 83, 90, 129
    food 51, 55, 62, 71–2, 76, 82, 83, 90
    housing 51, 52, 62, 71, 82, 83, 90
    justice 82, 83
    laws 73–6
    marriage 129
    medical care 62, 72, 82, 83, 90
    protest 55, 73, 76–9, 133
    punishment 52, 55, 72–3, 82, 83,
        86, 92
    recruitment 66–7
    restrictions 62, 70–1, 82
    sale 69
    working conditions 62, 72–3, 92
slave trade, abolition of 83–5
    by national companies 65–6
    factors aiding 87–9
    French slave trade abolished 91
    participants 61–2, 64–6
smugglers 17–18, 19, 20, 26, 37, 65,
    138, 141
social stratification 55, 62, 69–71
Society of West Indian Planters and
    Merchants of London 58
Somerset, James 84, 88
Sores, Jacques de 17
Spain, colonial administration 15
    efforts to prevent foreign incur-
        sions 28–30
    extent of decline in America 18–19
    monopoly challenged 16–18, 25
    monopoly in the West Indies 14–
        15
    restrictive trade regulations 16
Spanish Armada, defeat of in 1588 28
South Sea Company, and the slave
    trade 66
Stanley, Lord (Secretary of State for
    the Colonies) and Stipendiary
    Magistrates 95
Stipendiary Magistrates 90, 93
    appointment of 95
    assessment of their work 97–9,
        100, 102
    difficulties encountered 95–7
    functions and duties of 95–7
    salary 97

Strong, Joseph 84
Sugar Act of 1764 59
Sugar Duties Act (1846) 102
Sugar cane, and slavery 70–1
      competition to 57
      cultivation increased 48–9
      dangers to 44–5
      decline of 56–8, 94
      influence of 44
      method of cultivation and reaping 52–3
'sugar revolution' 49–51
      economic consequences of 49, 60
      political and military consequences of 50–1, 60
      social consequences of 49–50, 60

teaché 54
'The Society for Effecting the Abolition of the Slave Trade' 84, 88
tobacco, change to sugar 48–9
      reasons for cultivation 23, 46–8
Tobago 35, 37, 38, 39, 40, 41, 131
Togreman 23
trade regulations 45, 51, 56, 65
      British 139–41
      Spanish 137–9
trade rivalry 30, 34, 51, 139
treaty concessions by Spain 17–18, 20
Treaties, Aix-la-Chapelle (1748) 37, 66
      Amiens (1802) 41
      Antwerp (1609) 16–17, 29
      Breda (1667) 32
      Commerce (1750) 35
      London (1604) 29
      Madrid (1670) 24, 29
      Munster (1648) 29
      Nymwegen (1678) 29, 33
      Paris (1763) 38–9
      Paris (1814) 41
      Ratisbon (1680) 24
      Ryswick (1697) 24
      Tordesillas (1494) 13
      Utrecht (1713) 35, 36, 66
      Versailles (1783) 40
      Vervins (1598) 29
      Westminster (1654) 31
      Westminster (1674) 33
Trinidad 20, 41, 42, 85, 86, 95, 101, 115

Tromp, Admiral 27

Underhill, E. B. 119

Van Uytgeest 27
Venables, General 20
Vera Cruz 15, 138
Vice-Admiralty Court 141
Viceroy 15, 106, 108
voyages of Columbus, consequences 13–15
      influences behind 9–11
      results 12–13

Wars, American Independence (1776–1783) 34–5, 39–40, 51, 54, 56, 59, 143
      Anglo-American (1812–14) 42
      Anglo-Spanish (1585–1604) 26
      Austrian Succession (1740–48) 34–35, 37–8, 51, 54
      French Revolutionary and Napoleonic (1793–1815) 34–5, 41–2, 51, 54, 57, 143
      Jenkin's Ear (1739–48) 34–5, 37–8, 51, 54
      Seven Years' (1756–63) 34–5, 38–9, 51, 54
      Spanish Succession (1702–13) 20, 34–5, 36, 51, 54
      The Augsburg League (1689–97) 21
Warner, Sir Thomas 20, 22–3
Wedgewood Cameo 85
Wesley, Charles 88
'Western Design' 31, 140
West India Interest 58–9, 60, 89, 91, 92
whites, and Anglicans 130–1
      and Crown Colony Government 117
      and missionaries 131–2, 133
      and religious denominations 128–130
      classes of 69
      lack of vigilance 77
      special privileges of 70
Wilberforce, William 85, 88
Windward Islands 21
Windward Passage 23
Windward Squadron 15, 28, 29